TURNING ON MACHINES

TURNING ON MACHINES

How the Rise of Artificial Intelligence Will Rewire the Way We Work, Live, and Love

ZAC ENGLER

Cover by Zac Engler
Typesetting by JamesMonroeDesign.com
Production sponsored by BodhiAI.io

ISBN 13: 978-1-64343-463-6
Library of Congress Catalog Number: 2025918379
Printed in the United States of America
First Edition 2025
29 28 27 26 25 5 4 3 2 1

Beaver's Pond Press
526 Seventh Street West
Saint Paul, Minnesota 55102
(952) 829-8818
www.BeaversPondPress.com

To order, or to contact the author, visit zacengler.com.

To my family. You are the hidden force behind every word, my steady light when the world feels uncertain. Each of you, in your own way, helped me imagine a future with more intelligent machines and more connected humanity.

This book is a small return for the love, laughter, and hope you share with me every day.

CONTENTS

FOREWORD

It is truly an honor to receive a request to write a foreword for a book like this, in this particular space, at this specific time in history, and by a colleague whom I believe will make significant contributions to this industry during his tenure. That book is *Turning on Machines*, the time in history is the dawn of the VUCAD (virtual, uncertain, chaotic, ambiguous, and digital) world infused with artificial intelligence as a general-purpose technology, and my colleague is Zac Engler.

Zac is one of those unique individuals who improves people's lives just by being part of the group. Zac is a Thinking Man in the truest sense. He is traveled, cultured, educated, and experienced in a broad and deep way across a variety of disciplines that enable him to write a book of this stripe with justified authority. His inter-personal experience fusing the domains of technology, philosophy, business, consulting, culture, and education also undergird the wisdom required to produce a crafted work such as this one. The space of thinking machines will be enriched a little bit more because of this accession.

The book's theme assembles its elements from the **rise** of machines, humanity's **revolt** against them, and the eventual **reverence** for their capabilities. All of these facets are necessary given the nature of the VUCAD world that has changed the fundamental nature of machine intelligence, the human coping mechanism, society, and their future together.

The book begins, and quite appropriately so, with the topic of relationship-phase articulations *(Masters, Shepherds, Teachers, Peers, Partners,* and *Divergence)*, including their estimated timelines and the definitions of each epoch. This helps the reader understand how the relationship between humans and their synthetic counterparts becomes established and then evolves. This is crucial for developing a context in which to understand the gravity of our relationship with machines.

The **Rise** section of the book highlights the switching on of the machines and the marveling of humanity's creation of synthetic intelligence. In the **Revolt** section, our collective sentiments change notably for the worse as disruption spreads, jobs shift rapidly, institutions are challenged to adapt, and humans struggle and then resist what they cannot control. Poignantly, in the **Reverence** section, humans reimagine a future shaped by acceptance and the ensuing relationship between the organic and the synthetic. Each chapter is bolstered by history, culture, and the cameo appearance of a reality check or two.

This book is about chronicling the great paradigm shift humanity is in the midst of—how the relationship between humans and their egregore (synthetic creations, that is) begins, evolves, intertwines with, and eventually takes on a life of its own.

The book is as much a philosophical exploration as it is a historical, cultural, economic, and ideological journey with a bit of futurism interwoven for good measure against the backdrop of a new kind of digital transformation. For those influential in bridging the gap between the humanities and technology, this intellectual treatise is required reading.

—**Matthew R. Versaggi**, MS, MBA,
White House Presidential Innovation
Fellow in AI, Special Cohort of 2024,
Washington, DC

INTRODUCTION

A Mind for Machinery

For the first time in history, the machines we build are starting to think for themselves. Where does that leave us?

Most people move through life inside a single frame of awareness. They make choices, build careers, form relationships, and chase purpose, yet beneath it all, something ancient hums. The patterns of thoughts and behaviors we call "normal" were forged in the heat of survival. These instincts kept our ancestors alive, and now they trap us in the cycles of craving, fear, and reaction we see throughout society today.

Although the underpinnings of our ancient motivators remain, long ago there was a shift in *how* we survived. A shift that made us human. We learned to imagine what wasn't there.

We painted cave walls, shaped symbols into language, and built tools that could expand our reach. From sharpened stone to steam turbines, from copper wires to cloud networks, we moved beyond surviving the world, and we began shaping it. In doing so, we crossed a threshold: We became builders of systems, seekers of truth, and architects of the future.

Now another threshold is approaching. Artificial intelligence (AI) has entered our world not as a silent engine but as a voice that writes, thinks, interprets, and responds. Machines no longer wait for input; they generate it. They mirror our speech, analyze our desires, and anticipate our needs. They compose music, draft strategy, and sometimes surprise us.

Some say they're learning. Some say they're dreaming. At the very least, they are forcing us to ask deeper questions. This book is about that tension, about that wonder.

The Arc of Consciousness

Human consciousness evolved in layers. It began in the body, in the raw urgency of staying alive. It grew into emotion, the drive for connection and belonging. It expanded through reason into science, language, and control. And then, for a few, it softened again toward empathy, perspective, and meaning.

This arc of survival, emotion, intellect, and awareness is the silent engine behind civilization. Now it may be unfolding again . . . through us and in the machines we've created.

AI started in the shallow end of cognition: narrow tasks, pattern recognition, data processing. But it is learning at scale. It is evolving through feedback. It is building on itself. And with each advancement, it begins to resemble something more than machinery. It begins to resemble a mind.

What if our entire journey, from cave fires to code, from primal instinct to poetic insight, has been a preview of what machines are beginning to experience? What if, by watching them, we're learning something unexpected about ourselves?

Machines Learning? Why Bother?

Why would someone even want to consider my perspective? Because in 2016, before large language models were pervasive, before public discussion of autonomous agents, before viral image generation happened en masse, I laid out a forecast for AI development in my blog, Machines Learning, not by chasing headlines but by tracking raw computing power and applying patterns from previous tech revolutions.

I based my predictions of how fast AI would develop on TFLOPs (teraflops per second: how many trillions of math problems a computer can solve every second) benchmarks from the TOP500 supercomputer list by simply extending it forward. I used Moore's Law–style pattern matching and a healthy dose of skepticism to finalize my guess for when supercomputers would match the human brain in capability (not necessarily functionality). More importantly, I paired that exponential growth with human behavior: how people adapt (or don't) when the tools they rely on begin to outpace their own cognition.

That's how my six-phase framework was born, each phase reflecting not just what AI can do but what humans must become in response.

The Six Phases of Human–AI Evolution

1. **Masters (2014–2018):** Humans fully direct AI. We are the builders, the rule makers, and the gatekeepers.
2. **Shepherds (2018–2026):** We guide rather than command. AI gets smarter but still needs boundaries, tuning, and ethical feedback.
3. **Teachers (2026–2034):** We begin training AI agents like interns or apprentices, constantly improving them through iteration.
4. **Peers (2034–2038):** AI becomes capable of real collaboration—less tool, more teammate.
5. **Partners (2038–2042):** True synergy and companionship. AI connects to everything and extends human capability at scale.

6. **Divergence (2042–2046):** Society splits between interconnected users of AI and those left behind by choice, constraint, or resistance.

The transition from Masters to Shepherds around 2018 wasn't arbitrary—it marked a technological watershed. The "Attention Is All You Need" paper emerged in 2017. This paper introduced the Transformer, a new kind of computer program that understands sentences by using an "attention" mechanism to see how all the words relate to each other at once, rather than looking at them one by one like older programs. The year 2018 delivered its real impact though. GPT-1 launched that June, becoming the first large language model to exhibit emergent capabilities that surprised even its creators. Google's BERT followed in October, demonstrating a bidirectional understanding that felt almost humanlike.

It wasn't just raw computational power that made 2018 pivotal but the start of emergent behaviors: AI systems began doing things their creators never explicitly programmed them to do. Suddenly you couldn't simply command an AI with rigid rules; you had to learn to prompt, guide, and shepherd it toward desired outcomes. The relationship had fundamentally changed.

The point of my blog was that you don't need to fear the future, but you do need to understand it. That starts with seeing how the trajectory was always visible to those looking at the right indicators. I didn't just speculate; I set milestones. Now, nearly a decade later, here's how some of my projections have held up.

Forecasted Phase	Estimated Timeline	Reality Check
Masters	2014–2018	Accurate. AI was still narrow, rules-based, and used like any other software tool.
Shepherds	2018–2026	Happening now. Prompt engineers, human-in-the-loop training, and AI copilots are mainstream.
Teachers	2026–2034	Beginning early. Fine-tuning, feedback loops, and agentic workflows are emerging ahead of schedule.
Peers	2034–2038	On track. Some early signs in GPT-4-level agents and codesign tools.
Partners	2038–2042	Too early to evaluate, but we're trending toward human–machine parity.
Divergence	2042–2046	Still speculative, but early signs of division (access vs. exclusion, trust vs. fear) are obvious.

I don't have a PhD, but I understand technology's exponential growth and have been accurate in tracking it (sometimes too accurate) for the past decade. The forecast wasn't just an AI fear/hype machine. It was a way to recognize patterns, informed by experience in tech, hiring, and economic change. Furthermore, it was about getting ready. That's why I'm here now, sharing this story with anyone who is willing to listen to and consider it for themself and their future. The machines are turning on. Will we?

What This Book Is and Isn't

Turning On Machines is not a prediction of collapse or a blueprint for techno-utopia; it's a reflection. We will cover hypothetical future scenarios (both bleak and beautiful) of how AI will impact the way we work, live, and love. However, at the heart of this book is one guiding question: How will you navigate the rise of intelligent machines with clarity, courage, and consciousness?

We'll explore this question in three stages:

Stage One: Rise

We turn on the machines. AI begins as a tool, then grows into something more. We marvel at its potential even as it challenges our understanding of intelligence.

Stage Two: Revolt

Disruption spreads. Jobs shift, identities strain, and institutions struggle to adapt. In response, we turn on AI, resisting what we do not control.

Stage Three: Reverence

A turning point. We imagine a future not shaped by resistance but by relationships. Some partner with AI; others learn from it. A few are turned on and fall into obsession. All must choose how to adapt.

Each chapter grounds this arc in history, culture, and current reality. Alongside the ideas, you'll find spaces for reflection. These are moments to pause, look inward, and ask, "Where am I on this path? What am I resisting or reaching for?"

Why This Moment Matters

We are not just building tools; we are building mirrors.

The models we train, the systems we scale, and the choices we encode all reflect something back at us. This moment is a unique time for both technical progress and personal and societal presence. If AI continues to evolve, the question is: What will it become and how will we adapt to it?

This book is a guide through that shift, a bridge between awareness and action, and a call to meet the machines we're building with a deeper understanding of ourselves.

Welcome to your personal turning point in the largest paradigm shift humanity has ever experienced. Welcome to *Turning On Machines*.

PART I
RISE

CHAPTER 1

Rise, Revolt, Revere, Repeat

The only way to deal with an unfree world is to become so absolutely free that your very existence is an act of rebellion.

—Albert Camus

The Sharp Edge

Flint crouched by the riverbank, hands blistered from yesterday's hunt. The bone had shattered but not cleanly; too dull a rock, too much effort, not enough marrow. He watched his daughter as she squatted near the fire, striking one stone against another. Sparks flew. Tiny flakes scattered like scales. She had watched the older men before, but this was her first attempt alone.

He wanted to call her back, tell her to leave it to the skilled ones. But then she held up a perfectly shaped flake with edges so fine it shimmered in the light. Flint blinked. His daughter went beyond copying the old shape and made something new. She held it differently, using a smaller stone to chip it finer.

That evening, the meat came easier. The marrow sweeter. Her edge worked better than his ever had. The others noticed. She said nothing, but Flint saw it in her eyes: pride . . . and something else. Curiosity, maybe. Or danger. Because now tools were more than things for surviving. They were about changing everything.

Stone Tools: Our First Technological Leap

The preceding scene, while imagined, reflects what archaeologists now believe about the early human relationship with technology. When our distant mammalian ancestors first picked up a rough-edged stone to crack open a nut or carve a piece of wood, they unknowingly ignited a spark that would blaze through the rest of our existence. It's fascinating to think about how those simple actions by our very distant relatives paved the way for the mechanized world we navigate today. When we started our relationship with machines, life was all about survival.

Every sunrise brought new challenges, and innovation was necessary to make it to the next one. Roughly 2.6 million years ago, our ancestors in East Africa began crafting tools through a deliberate process known as knapping—striking stone to produce sharp flakes. More than casual breakages, these were intentional, repeatable designs. At sites like Kathu Pan 1 in South Africa and Olduvai Gorge in Tanzania, researchers have found extensive evidence of early hominins using these tools to butcher animals, scrape hides, and extract nutrient-rich marrow from bones (Highland 2017).

The use of stone tools allowed early humans to transcend the limits of their own biology. With relatively little physical strength or natural defense, they survived by transforming their environment. This marked a cognitive leap: The tools themselves were evidence of coordination, and more importantly, planning and spatial reasoning. Over time, the tools became more complex. Archaeological layers show an evolution from general-purpose tools to specialized ones, each suited to a distinct task.

What's even more remarkable is how these tools shaped early society. Evidence from tool-making sites suggests that certain individuals were more skilled than others. This led to an informal kind of specialization, with some focusing on hunting, others on foraging, and a select few on developing advanced tool-making knowledge. Work roles, in their earliest form, began here.

Teaching and innovation also played a key role. Sites show refined tools and experimental forms, implying that learning happened through observation, trial, and mentorship. Innovation didn't flow only from master to student. Some of the most notable breakthroughs likely came from newcomers who dared to try something different (Wilkins 2020).

As with many technologies, not everyone benefited equally. Communities with access to high-quality materials (like obsidian or flint) had clear advantages. Over generations, these advantages compounded exponentially, shaping survival outcomes. In contrast, groups with inferior materials or slower adoption faced real disadvantages. This early divide foreshadowed the exponential technological inequalities that would echo through every age to follow.

Over time, sharpened stones evolved from survival tools into cultural artifacts. They marked identity, skill, and even status within the group. Some researchers suggest that gender roles may have begun to form around the types of tasks individuals performed, with women playing a larger role in gathering and fine-motor tasks (including tool production) than was once assumed.

The Historical Edge: Stone Tools

When our ancestors struck stone against stone, they revealed the timeless formula for navigating disruption: Curiosity beats expertise. Archaeological evidence shows that successful toolmakers weren't following rigid patterns but constantly experimenting with new angles and materials, just as today's AI winners iterate relentlessly with prompts and approaches.

The biggest breakthroughs came from outsiders who dared to try something different, unburdened by conventional wisdom about how stones "should" be shaped. This mirrors how nonprogrammers today discover revolutionary AI applications that experts miss.

Most sobering is the compound inequality: Communities near high-quality obsidian made better tools, period. Their advantages multiplied exponentially over generations, foreshadowing how early AI adopters aren't just slightly ahead but are building capabilities that compound daily.

Mastery of Fire: Elemental Technology

Evidence in the archaeological record shows the first hearths appeared nearly four hundred thousand years ago. At sites like Gesher Benot Ya'aqov and Wonderwerk Cave, scientists have found layered ash deposits, burned wood, and bones blackened at their edges—evidence of the kind of burn that doesn't come from a lightning strike or a passing spark. This was intentional. Like a treasure, fire was discovered and then kept very close.

What started as warmth became strategy. Meat softened. Starch broke down. Bacteria died. Bodies spent less energy on digestion. That energy went somewhere else. Some believe it went to the brain. Richard Wrangham (2009) argues that cooked food sparked an evolutionary leap, which opened up resources that helped our minds grow faster, stronger, and to some degree stranger.

Fire also changed how we experience time. There were hours now, not just days. People stayed awake after the sun went down. They sat together. Spoke more. Learned how to hold still long enough to wonder. You can't pass down a story when you're sprinting through forests or fleeing a predator. Fire gave us pause . . . and in that pause, memory took shape.

But fire was never simple. It needed to be fed. Managed. Watched. It slipped. It spread. It reminded us often that this tool was a guest that could turn violent.

Some resisted. Nomadic groups who valued motion saw fire as a weight to be carried. It demanded routine, fuel, and space. You couldn't carry flame easily across miles. And you couldn't rely on it when the rains came. Some may have resisted because of what it revealed:

that survival might come with compromise, and that new technology was less a gift than a wager.

In Australia and sub-Saharan Africa, traces of ancient burn patterns suggest that early humans were already managing land, clearing brush, drawing animals with ashes, and releasing nutrients into the soil (Bird et al. 2008). Our use of fire quickly transitioned from cooking to sculpting the wild.

The Historical Edge: Fire

Fire's four-hundred-thousand-year-old lesson teaches us that discovery and dedication work in tandem. Evidence reveals that successful fire keepers mastered both the spark and the daily ritual (feeding, managing, and watching their flames with unwavering commitment). While some nomadic groups found fire's demands incompatible with their mobile lifestyle, communities that integrated its requirements gained compound returns: cooked food that freed brain-building calories, evening hours that birthed storytelling and knowledge transfer, and eventually the power to reshape entire landscapes through controlled burns (Wrangham 2009; Bird et al. 2008).

Today's AI success follows this same pattern: Thriving comes from building daily workflows, maintaining prompt libraries, and treating AI as a powerful force that requires ethical boundaries and constant oversight. Those who view AI's learning curve as too steep echo ancient nomads who prioritized familiar freedoms, perhaps not yet seeing how technological integration (however demanding) often catalyzes our next evolutionary leap.

Agriculture: The First Exponential Engine

The story of agriculture is the story of our first truly exponential technology. It begins slowly and then takes off rapidly. A few plants grew where seeds had fallen. Some stayed to tend them. Then the plants came back the next season. In time, the wait became a rhythm that built into a crescendo.

Communities settling near fertile river valleys about twelve thousand years ago began to cultivate plants and domesticate animals, a monumental shift known as the Neolithic Revolution (Moore et al. 2000). This didn't happen overnight as an isolated change but as a gradual transition from nomadic hunter-gatherers to settled farmers in various regions around the world.

In the Fertile Crescent, favorable climate and geography facilitated the domestication of wheat, barley, sheep, and goats (Naithani 2021). In East Asia, rice cultivation began along the Yangtze River, while in Mesoamerica, maize, beans, and squash were domesticated (LibreTexts 2020). Simple tools like digging sticks evolved into plows, and with the help of domesticated animals, farming became exponentially more efficient (Smith 1995).

As with use of fire, once people settled into agricultural societies, time changed shape again. Days were no longer dictated by movement but by tasks like planting, weeding, harvesting, and storing crops. Memory extended beyond the individual. Tools became specialized. Food, once eaten on the move, sat in storehouses under guard.

Surplus and seasons offered new possibilities. With more than enough food, some people began to plan, direct, and protect. Roles fractured and specialized: labor, leadership, recordkeeping, enforcement. It didn't happen all at once. But eventually communities transformed into societal systems.

These systems carried weight. The land needed more than seeds. It needed irrigation, boundaries, and protection. Crops demanded tools that stone couldn't sustain. So, ore was drawn from the earth: copper, then bronze. Metallurgy followed farming like a shadow follows flame, intentionally and hungrily. Necessity breeds invention, and that was the next logical step.

The act of staying in place led to new burdens as well as new solutions. Heavy yields led to the invention of the wheel—first in carts to transport goods, then in the potter's wheel to shape storage vessels, and eventually in water wheels that harnessed energy to move and lift water. You might think these were stand-alone inventions, but they really belonged to a growing web of human interdependence. Looking back, you can see that innovation was simply one link pulling the next.

Dr. Melinda Zeder (2008) describes this shift as a cascade of reasoning. The early farmers transitioned from surviving to scaffolding new styles of existence. Furthermore, as Dr. Roy Casagranda (2018) argues, once calories could be stored, culture began to evolve faster than the human body ever had (or could). Physical limitations stepped back. Story stepped in. With biology in the back seat, so began our exponential climb.

This new way of life wasn't without challenges. Farming required hard labor that figuratively and literally tied people to the land. Dependence on crops made societies vulnerable to droughts and pests. Social hierarchies emerged, sometimes leading to inequality and conflict over resources. While agriculture allowed for population growth and technological advancements, it also led to health issues from a less varied diet and the spread of diseases in denser populations (Cohen and Armelagos 1984). Interestingly enough, these challenges would ignite further innovations in health care and medicine.

Some groups clearly resisted this new sedentary lifestyle, preferring the mobility and freedom of a hunter-gatherer existence (Kelly 2013). The transformation of landscapes through farming led to deforestation and soil depletion, impacting ecosystems for generations to come (Montgomery 2007). Agricultural societies often dominated or displaced hunter-gatherer groups, leading to cultural and economic disparities that still echo into our modern times.

The Historical Edge: Agriculture

Agriculture's twelve-thousand-year-old wisdom reveals how exponential technologies reward patient builders over quick harvesters. The Neolithic farmers who thrived understood compound returns: Planting seeds meant accepting delayed gratification, but those who mastered the rhythm of seasons built surpluses that changed everything (Diamond 1997). With stored calories came specialization (some became planters; others became builders, leaders, or recordkeepers) creating the cascade where innovation developed from one link pulling the next, from farming to metallurgy to the wheel and beyond.

Today's AI adopters face the same exponential curve: Early experiments feel slow and uncertain, but those investing in building long-term capability watch their efforts compound as each use case unlocks another. The hunter-gatherer groups who rejected agriculture's constraints for familiar freedoms mirror today's AI skeptics who prefer traditional workflows, perhaps not yet seeing how these insights apply to our moment: Once we can store and multiply cognitive capacity through AI, our capabilities evolve faster than our biology ever could.

Printing the World Anew

The printing press emerged from centuries of slow ingenuity, tectonic progress bubbling up across continents. This came in the form of ceramic type in China, wood-block engravings in Korea, and monastic scriptoria in Europe. Eventually the earth shook when Johannes Gutenberg married movable metal type with a modified wine press in the German city of Mainz around 1440. That's when something fundamental changed: Duplication became scalable, and with it, both knowledge and authority became portable.

By 1500, over two hundred cities had printing presses. Over twenty million volumes had been produced—more than the entire scribal output of the prior millennium (Febvre and Martin 2010). For the first time, ideas could travel at the speed of a lithographer's hands.

Elizabeth Eisenstein (1980, 71), the preeminent historian of print, argues that Gutenberg's press initiated a revolution in "fixity" and "dissemination," meaning ideas no longer decayed with time or geography; they could be preserved, replicated, and circulated. Maps became more accurate. Scientific diagrams went from being regional to being continental. Authority could now be contested with evidence rather than obedience.

The Reformation is impossible to understand without the press. Martin Luther's ninety-five theses were copied and printed in dozens of towns across the Holy Roman Empire, reaching thousands in days. Luther understood the power of timing and translation. His tracts in vernacular German found both unsuspecting readers and restless ones (Johns 1998). This newfound literacy was both liberating and highly volatile, kicking off some of the bloodiest wars in premodern history.

Concurrently, the same machines that reproduced Galileo's observations also spread pseudoscience and moral panic. Early print culture teemed with forgeries, plagiarisms, and unverified claims. Ironically, it was a media ecosystem not unlike today's internet. Misinformation didn't emerge with an algorithm; it rode in with the printing press (Johns 1998).

Even Gutenberg's workshop faced controversy over fraud and financial disputes (Man 2002). As early as 1470, officials in Paris expressed concern over the teeming volumes of lies in popular literature, such as newsletters, cheap pamphlets, and fabricated prophecies that preyed on fear more than facts (Eisenstein 1980).

The Historical Edge: Printing Press

The printing press revolution teaches us that technological disruption rewards those who master both creation and curation. When Gutenberg's invention spread, the winners understood how to navigate the new ecosystem of dissemination. Martin Luther succeeded by combining three insights: timing his message perfectly, translating complex ideas into vernacular, and recognizing that authority now flowed from evidence rather than position. The same chaos that enabled scientific breakthroughs also unleashed forgeries, plagiarisms, and volumes of lies that drove valid cause for concern.

Today's AI pioneers face a similar duality: Those who thrive combine rapid content creation with careful verification, adapt AI outputs for specific audiences rather than accepting generic responses, and understand that in a world where anyone can generate expert-sounding content, credibility comes from consistent quality and transparent methodology. The printing-press era's deepest lesson echoes through our ChatGPT age: When information democratizes overnight, success belongs to those who become trusted filters in the flood.

Industrial Revolution: Machines for Muscles

The printing press let knowledge travel. The scientific method gave it discipline. Together, they made knowledge replicable and progress repeatable. The late eighteenth century marked a seismic shift in human history. As steam and steel replaced soil and sweat, the Industrial Revolution propelled work into the age of mechanization. What once required hand tools, human labor, and seasonal rhythms became the domain of machines—relentless, tireless, and precise.

James Watt's steam engine, developed in the 1760s, fueled this transformation. Factories and locomotives replaced farms and footpaths. Workers moved to cities, learning to operate and repair machines that made their previous skills obsolete (Mokyr 1990).

The power loom, patented by Edmund Cartwright in 1785, disrupted the textile industry. Skilled weavers faced unemployment or lower wages as cloth was now produced faster and cheaper. Some rioted; the Luddites famously smashed machines in protest (Binfield 2004). Others retrained and took factory jobs, though often at diminished status.

Railroads and steamships displaced entire transportation sectors. Coachmen, canal workers, and horse breeders either adapted by joining the railroad boom or watched their trades fade. Similarly, the telegraph (1830s) and telephone (1876) upended communication work. Mail couriers and telegraphers retrained as switchboard operators or line technicians, ushering in new forms of technical and customer-facing labor (Allen 2017).

Electric lighting, made practical by Thomas Edison in 1879, extinguished the need for candles and gas lamps. It birthed a new electrical industry (installers, technicians, and night-shift laborers) while stretching workdays and reshaping human schedules (Wilkinson 2025).

As machines grew in power, so too did inequality. Wages fell, child labor surged, and workers toiled under punishing conditions. Labor unions rose in response, demanding rights, safety, and dignity. Meanwhile, industrialized nations leveraged their advances to colonize and extract resources from others, sowing seeds of global wealth disparity.

But amid all this upheaval, the human mind remained irreplaceable. Machines could augment, not outthink. That was the unspoken pact of progress.

The Historical Edge: Industrial Revolution

The Industrial Revolution's harshest lesson resonates through every disruption since: Survival belongs to the reinventors. When Watt's steam engine and Cartwright's power loom obliterated entire professions, those who thrived shared a ruthless pragmatism about identity. Skilled weavers who transitioned to factory work, coach drivers who became railroad engineers, and telegraph operators who retrained as telephone line technicians understood that clinging to obsolete expertise guaranteed obsolescence. The real winners spotted opportunity where others saw only loss.

Today's AI disruption demands the same professional shape-shifting: paralegals becoming prompt engineers, copywriters mastering AI-assisted storytelling, and analysts enhancing rather than competing with machine intelligence. The Luddites who smashed looms in protest were justified in their actions, but those who asked, "What new role can I fill?" wrote the playbook for every technological transition since. The Industrial Revolution's unspoken pact, "Machines can augment our effectiveness," holds true for AI: Those who position themselves as the irreplaceable human element in human-machine partnerships inherit the future.

Dawn of Computing: From Mechanical Muscles to Electronic Encephalons

The origins of the computer on your desk or the one in your pocket can be traced back to the early nineteenth century when Charles Babbage envisioned the Difference Engine, a mechanical calculator designed to automate the production of mathematical tables. By 1837, he proposed the more ambitious Analytical Engine, a programmable device that introduced the core components of modern computing: a central processor (the "mill"), memory (the "store"), and input/output systems (Swade 2000).

Ada Lovelace, a mathematician who worked closely with Babbage, translated and expanded on an article about the Analytical Engine in 1843. Her notes included what many consider the first computer algorithm, and she presciently predicted that machines could eventually manipulate symbols to create music or art—not just perform math (Toole 1992).

Fast-forward to 1936, when Alan Turing introduced the concept of the Turing machine, a theoretical framework that defined the principles of algorithmic computation. Though abstract, it laid the groundwork for understanding the limits and potential of any computing system (Turing 1936).

During World War II, Turing applied those ideas practically at Bletchley Park, developing the Bombe—an electromechanical machine used to decrypt Nazi Germany's Enigma codes. His work proved critical to the Allied war effort and positioned computation as a strategic tool in both warfare and intelligence (Hodges 1983).

The age of electronic computing began in 1945 with the completion of the Electronic Numerical Integrator and Computer (ENIAC) in the United States—one of the first general-purpose electronic computers. Unlike earlier mechanical machines, ENIAC could rapidly perform complex calculations using vacuum tubes (McCartney 1999).

In 1951, the Universal Automatic Computer I (UNIVAC I) became the first commercially available computer, delivered to the United States Census Bureau. Built by J. Presper Eckert and John Mauchly, UNIVAC I marked the shift of computing from military and academic domains into business and government, handling both numerical and textual data (Ceruzzi 2003).

From mechanical gears to programmable machines, from theoretical models to commercial systems, this early lineage ignited the Digital Revolution—shaping the intelligent tools we now live alongside every day.

The Historical Edge: Early Computing

Computing's revolutionary lesson centers on those who saw beyond the obvious. When Babbage built his Analytical Engine and when Lovelace glimpsed something others missed, they connected unseen but predictable dots. Turing embodied another winning pattern, transforming abstract theory into mechanized computation. The true accelerant came when visionaries recognized computing's moment to leap domains, from military secrets into business tools, while collaborative pairs (Babbage-Lovelace, Eckert-Mauchly) consistently outpaced solo inventors.

Today's AI winners follow this playbook: They envision applications beyond chatbots (seeing AI as creative partner, research assistant, business strategist), bridge the gap between AI theory and practical implementation, recognize when AI tools mature enough to transform their industry, and build collaborative networks rather than hoard knowledge. The computing pioneers teach us that technological revolutions reward expanded imagination and strategic timing over technical mastery alone.

It's quite poetic, actually. This is the pattern of all transformation: Fear and wonder dance together until purpose leads.

Skeptics give us guardrails. Believers give us wings. Both perspectives are necessary for progress. When you introduce something that fundamentally changes how humans work, live, and think, you need voices asking, "What could go wrong?" alongside voices asking, "What could go right?"

Every revolution starts with a question nobody thought to ask. Today, we stand at another threshold. The machines are smarter, the stakes are higher, and the real question remains: Will we find balance?

What do we want these partnerships to create? What problems are we solving together? What future are we building hand in hand with our digital companions?

The answer lives in us, in our choices, and in our shared vision for tomorrow.

Big History Reflections: Human–Machine Coevolution

Throughout our history, tools and machines have been more than just objects; they've been partners in our progress. Each advancement has brought us new opportunities and new challenges. We've had to learn how to use these innovations and how to responsibly integrate them into our lives.

Looking back, it's clear that our story is one of constant innovation. From sharpened stones to intelligent machines, each new chapter has been powered by curiosity and necessity that aim to overcome obstacles, improve our circumstances, and help us explore the unknown. Only by working together are we able to fully account for what makes us human and where machines can help us stay true to ourselves.

So, you see, we've coevolved with machines all along because machines are ultimately the products of our minds. As we move forward, the tools we create will continue to shape us just as we shape them. The challenges may be new, but the spirit with which we face them by working together remains the same. Now we must prepare to go beyond the technology itself and shape our collective focus on how we choose to use it and how we let it influence our lives, our work, and our world.

Self-Reflection: The Human–Machine Ascent

Understanding Our Roles as Technology Evolves

Think about how tools and technology have shaped the world around you. Just as our ancestors moved from stone tools to metal ones, we've seen incredible shifts in our own lifetimes. Consider your industry or field of work within the following self-guided contemplations.

Personal Inventory

- List the major technological changes that have impacted your profession.
- How have these advancements changed the way tasks are performed?

Questions to Consider

- Are there tools you rely on today that didn't exist a decade ago?
- How have you adapted to these changes?
- What skills did you need to learn to keep up?

By examining the evolution within your own sphere, you can gain insights into how progress unfolds and how it affects us on a personal level.

Embracing Self-Awareness and Adaptability

Change can be unsettling, but it's also an opportunity for growth. Just as our ancestors had to adapt to new tools and environments, we too face the challenge of staying nimble in a rapidly shifting world.

Assess Your Adaptability

- Recall a time when you had to learn a new technology or process.
- How did you feel during that transition?
- What strategies did you use to overcome any hurdles?

Action Steps

- Identify an area where you might be resisting change.
- Set a small, achievable goal to explore this area; maybe it's trying out a new software or attending a workshop.
- Celebrate small victories as you step out of your comfort zone.

By fostering a mindset of continuous learning and flexibility, you can begin to position yourself in a way that allows you to navigate future changes with confidence.

Prompt the Machine 1

Add this prompt to your favorite large language model to dive deeper into the subject matter with AI:

"I've just reflected on how past tools shaped human history, and now I'm curious about my own story. Based on what you know about how humans adapted to fire, farming, the wheel, and the printing press, can you help me map my own technology arc? Ask me questions, one at a time, to help me identify which tech changes have most reshaped my work, values, and identity, and where I may be resisting or embracing the next leap forward."

CHAPTER 2
The AI Surge

We can only see a short distance ahead, but we can see plenty there that needs to be done.

—Alan Turing

Control, Alter, Delete

A girl in Manila whispers into her phone at 3:16 a.m. She isn't calling anyone. She's speaking to an AI that calls her "sunbeam" and remembers everything she's said for the past forty days.

A man in Berlin clicks "publish." He's just uploaded a ten-thousand-word technical paper on a breakthrough in protein folding—written almost entirely by GPT-4.

At the same moment, a CEO in San Francisco lays off fifty employees. Most of their responsibilities are now handled by AI-powered dashboards, data agents, and automated customer-support workflows. He thanks them all on Zoom. The call lasts seven minutes.

None of these events are considered remarkable, but they are the bellwether of something new. This is the AI surge.

The Dawn of Learning Systems

Alan Turing (1950, 433) famously asked, "Can machines think?" It's a question that planted the seed for a revolution in intelligence itself. Over the decades, that question has evolved into a movement to push the boundaries of what machines can do, enabling them not only to solve problems but to learn. Today, the fruits of this inquiry are transforming industries and redefining the limits of human achievement.

In the mid-twentieth century, as colossal computers dominated entire rooms, visionaries like Turing dared to imagine machines capable of mimicking human thought. His seminal work, including the now-famous Turing Test, was a blueprint for AI expectations and a challenge to see if machines could ever mirror human intelligence in conversation.

The term *artificial intelligence* was formally coined in 1956 during the Dartmouth Conference, a gathering of thinkers inspired by Turing's vision. Early breakthroughs like the Logic Theorist, a program capable of proving mathematical theorems, offered tantalizing glimpses of machines reasoning like humans. Yet these initial successes were fleeting; the challenges of replicating human adaptability proved monumental. Over the following decades, limited computational power and overly simplistic algorithms slowed progress, leading to an AI winter, a period of waning interest and investment.

From Rules to Learning: The Machine Learning Breakthrough

What turned the tide wasn't teaching machines what to think but teaching them how to learn. Arthur Samuel's concept of machine learning in the late 1950s marked the shift. This approach allowed computers to improve their performance based on data rather than rigid programming. By the 1980s, the introduction of back-propagation (a method for refining artificial neural networks) enabled machines to identify patterns and adjust accordingly, laying the groundwork for modern AI.

Fast forward to today: Vast datasets and powerful computational tools fuel deep learning, allowing algorithms to refine themselves at unprecedented speeds. The ImageNet competition in 2012 marked a watershed moment, where the AlexNet neural networks shattered records in image recognition. Suddenly machines could interpret and process visual data with accuracy that rivaled human capabilities. The leap was transcendental and transformational.

Landmark Moments in AI's Rise

While deep learning powered remarkable advancements, certain milestones demonstrated AI's potential to the world.

Deep Blue (1997): IBM's chess-playing computer defeated Garry Kasparov, the reigning world champion. This wasn't merely a triumph in logic; it was a declaration that machines could master strategy, once thought exclusive to human intelligence.

Watson on Jeopardy! (2011): IBM's Watson outperformed human champions in one of the most complex natural language tasks; synthesizing vast data and responding to nuanced prompts in real time.

AlphaGo's Victory (2016): Google DeepMind's AlphaGo beat Lee Sedol, a master of the ancient strategy game Go. With more potential moves than atoms in the universe, Go was long thought to be uncrackable by machines. Yet AlphaGo not only won but displayed a kind of intuition that astonished experts.

ChatGPT 3.5 Launched (2022): OpenAI's breakout hit exploded into mainstream use and quickly became the fastest-growing internet service ever, reaching one hundred million users just two short months after launch. Other chatbots have followed, but this moment marked a sea change in how the world interacts with AI.

DeepSeek-R1 Launched (2025): The ChatGPT competitor was noteworthy for its advanced reasoning capabilities and its development at a relatively low cost compared to similar models. R1's release drew controversy, and its rise over bigger, more established competitors has been considered "the first shot" in what many see as a global war for AI dominance.

How Machines Learn: A Closer Look

At the heart of AI's advancements are artificial neural networks, complex algorithms modeled after the human brain. These networks learn by identifying patterns in data and refining their "understanding" through repeated exposure. Techniques like reinforcement learning, which rewards algorithms for achieving optimal results, simulate a kind of trial-and-error learning that mirrors human decision-making.

Breakthroughs such as Transformer models helped revolutionize language processing. By analyzing entire sentences and their contexts, Transformers enable AI to generate humanlike text, as seen in tools like OpenAI's GPT (generative pretrained Transformer) models. These innovations helped to redefine how machines interact with language, making them invaluable for tasks ranging from content creation to customer service.

But this is just the beginning. Regardless of what AI type is being developed and how fast it's accelerating, the real area of concern is how AI is entering the workforce.

Transforming Work: AI's Expanding Horizons

Industries across the board are reaping the rewards of AI integration, creating unparalleled opportunities for those willing to adapt.

Health Care: AI-driven advancements accelerate drug discovery and precision diagnostics, enabling health-care professionals to deliver faster and more accurate treatments. For those in medical fields, embracing AI-driven diagnostics positions them as vital connectors between cutting-edge technology and patient care.

Transportation: Autonomous vehicles promise safer roads and more efficient traffic management. Logistics experts and urban planners who familiarize themselves with AI-driven logistics networks gain a strategic advantage, enhancing their value as orchestrators of complex automated systems.

Finance: AI-powered tools rapidly detect fraudulent activities and inform predictive investment strategies. Professionals skilled at interpreting and leveraging AI-driven financial insights become indispensable, transforming data into actionable decisions.

Agriculture: Smart sensors and drones using AI significantly boost productivity and sustainability. Agricultural professionals who adopt these technologies not only enhance yields but also position themselves as leaders in the emerging smart-agriculture sector.

Manufacturing: Predictive maintenance and robotic precision drastically reduce downtime and enhance productivity. Workers and engineers who understand and manage AI-driven manufacturing technologies are essential for seamless, efficient operations.

Each advancement of AI into the workplace underscores the importance of adaptability, turning professionals into key drivers of AI integration rather than passive observers.

The Human Role in an AI World

With machines learning and adapting at unprecedented rates, you might wonder: If AI can do everything, where do people fit in? The answer lies in collaboration. While AI excels in pattern recognition and data analysis, humans bring creativity, empathy, and judgment, qualities no algorithm can replicate . . . yet.

Modern professionals can take a page from historic technological disruptions; the key to thriving in an AI-driven world is adaptability. In the coming chapters, we'll explore this topic further through the lens of employability, automation-resistant roles, and a mix of job landscape scenarios.

A New Frontier of Intelligence

AI has brought us to an inflection point. What began as a quest to mimic human thought has evolved into a force that surpasses it in speed and scale. The opportunities are immense, and so are the challenges. As machines continue to learn, grow, and integrate into our lives, the journey becomes one of what we can do together.

How will AI shape our future? How will we choose to shape it collaboratively? Who will revolt against it? Who will revere it? How might an artificial superintelligence takeoff happen? Why should we act now to create strategies and tactics for adjusting to life with AI? Let's find out.

Self-Reflection: Accelerating AI

Understanding AI's Role in Our Lives

Artificial intelligence is now a part of everyday reality. From voice assistants to health-care recommendations, AI touches many aspects of our lives.

Explore Your Interactions with AI

- Make a list of all the ways you engage with AI technologies daily.
- Consider both obvious and subtle examples, like that smart thermostat adjusting the temperature or facial recognition algorithms at airport security.

Questions to Consider

- How has AI improved your day-to-day experiences?
- Are there areas where AI feels intrusive or concerning to you?
- What misconceptions might you have had about AI before recognizing its presence in your life?

By becoming more aware of how AI integrates into your routine, you can better understand its impact and potential.

Preparing for an AI-Integrated Future

As AI continues to evolve, it's essential to think about how we can coexist and thrive alongside it.

Identify Opportunities for Growth

- Look at your professional field and pinpoint where AI is making inroads.
- Are there skills you can acquire to stay ahead of the curve?

Action Steps

- Choose one aspect of AI that interests you—perhaps machine learning, low-code automations, agentic workflows, or ethical considerations.
- Find resources like online courses, articles, or local workshops to deepen your knowledge.
- Connect with others who share your interest to build a supportive network.

Embracing AI doesn't mean surrendering to the machines; it's about enhancing your capabilities and staying relevant in a changing landscape.

Prompt the Machine 2

Add this prompt to your favorite large language model to dive deeper into the subject matter with AI:

"I'm realizing that AI is woven into more of my life than I thought. Can you help me unpack where it's already affecting me, both directly and subtly? Walk me through a day in my life and ask questions, one at a time, to surface how AI might be showing up in ways I've overlooked or underestimated."

CHAPTER 3

Navigating the Tides of Transformation

The best way to predict the future is to invent it.

—Alan Kay

A Job That Wasn't There Before

Maria wasn't job hunting. She was simply helping her nephew research potential careers for a class assignment. But curiosity got the better of her. One click became another, and soon Maria found herself experimenting with an AI-driven marketing tool.

Initially, using AI felt uncomfortable—almost unethical, like getting credit for someone else's work. Yet gradually, the discomfort transformed into intrigue, a strategic game akin to playing chess with a tireless partner. Her skillful collaboration with AI quickly caught her manager's attention, leading to a newly created position for

Maria—and for an entirely new breed of worker: one who seamlessly thinks alongside machines.

Meanwhile, in another city, James, a small-business owner, leveraged AI differently. He used it to refine job descriptions, efficiently pair freelancers with projects, and secure valuable client contracts. He didn't want to replace employees; he wanted to reclaim precious time.

Quietly, across industries and continents, change was occurring. It hadn't turned into an upheaval or a perfect solution yet, just a subtle yet profound redefinition of human work.

Societal Shifts and Industry Impact: The New Fabric of Work

AI is the defining technology of our modern-day evolution. As self-learning systems begin to evolve themselves, their impact ripples across industries, society, and our understanding of what it means to work and thrive as a species. Yet with great change comes great uncertainty, and humanity finds itself at a crossroads. Do we let these technologies shape us, or do we actively shape them?

When AI steps into a workspace, it brings more than just efficiency; it redefines roles, relationships, and the very nature of productivity. Imagine a logistics company where human drivers collaborate with autonomous delivery drones, or a hospital where nurses use AI-powered diagnostics to prioritize care. What was once pure theory is now unfolding in real time.

In manufacturing, predictive algorithms ensure machines operate seamlessly, cutting downtime to near zero. In finance, AI sifts through millions of transactions to identify fraud as it occurs. Even creative fields aren't untouched: Generative models design clothing, compose music, and draft movie scripts. But as machines become capable of performing tasks once reserved for skilled professionals, a pressing question looms: Where do we fit in?

The shift is profound. Workers in repetitive, process-driven roles are the first to feel the pinch. Automation replaces tasks that once required hours of manual labor. However, adaptation is the human superpower. Consider how factory workers displaced by mechanization during the Industrial Revolution learned to operate and maintain the very machines that replaced their old jobs. Today's equivalent lies in acquiring skills to collaborate with technology rather than compete against it.

For you, this could mean investing in skills that machines cannot easily replicate: creative problem-solving, emotional intelligence, leadership, physical care, and adaptability. The questions then transition from "What job should I get?" to "How can I make myself indispensable in an AI-augmented world?"

Navigating the AI Frontier: How to Future-Proof Your Career

You don't have to race machines. You have to think with them or differentiate yourself from what they're good at. That means using judgment, empathy, and physical touch. The most important edge comes from what you notice other humans needing, what assumptions you question, and how you pursue that which only a human can do well.

Despite impressive advancements, certain roles remain inherently human, safeguarded by trust, complexity, and authentic interaction.

Care-Based Professions: Health-care roles, childcare, and elder care demand trust and emotional intelligence—qualities that resist replication by algorithms.

Licensed Trades: Professions such as electricians and plumbers require practical skills, experiential judgment, and nuanced human decision-making.

Government and Regulatory Roles: Judges, auditors, legislators—these roles hinge upon ethical decision-making and human accountability protected by law.

Experiential Jobs: Roles centered around human connection like adventure guides, culinary artisans, and performing artists offer experiences fundamentally human at their core.

Understanding this delineation is crucial; automation targets predictability, but humanity thrives in complexity, nuance, and empathy. The future rewards capability over credentials. Career durability now demands active cultivation of distinctly human skills, paired with a deep understanding of AI tools. Three vital capacities emerge:

Strategic Judgment: Knowing precisely when to automate tasks and when to maintain human oversight. Professionals skilled at asking insightful, probing questions (not just providing answers) gain significant leverage.

Social Intelligence: Empathy, nuanced communication, and emotional resilience remain irreplaceable. These qualities transform routine interactions into meaningful exchanges.

AI Literacy: Active engagement with AI systems, from understanding biases and limitations to orchestrating their integration into complex tasks, becomes essential.

The future invites professionals to reconsider their roles proactively, shifting the question from "Will my job exist?" to "How can my uniquely human strengths be amplified by AI?" This reframing turns uncertainty into strategic clarity, positioning you as an indispensable architect of an AI-first future because, let's face it, you won't always be in control of who stays and who goes at the company you work for.

The Efficiency Trap: Automate and Eliminate

Many executive teams fall into the trap of viewing automation as an all-or-nothing solution: automate tasks, shift workloads to fewer employees, and eventually cut head count. While this approach may yield short-term savings, it carries serious long-term risks. As Simon Sinek (2019) would say, it's a finite tactic in an infinite game.

Overloaded employees face burnout and disengagement, and the loss of experienced staff erodes critical knowledge and problem-solving skills. Relying too heavily on automation also stifles creativity and limits a company's ability to nimbly adapt to market changes.

Instead, what if efficiency led to growth, not downsizing? This is where work trifurcation creates lasting value, balancing automation with human ingenuity.

Understanding the Trifurcation

So what exactly is work trifurcation? Here's an outline of how work can be delineated into new categories to optimize role-based tasks for the appropriate resource (human or AI).

AI-Driven Tasks and Roles: These are repetitive or data-intensive activities that AI agents can manage entirely, enhancing efficiency and reducing human error. Copywriting, project invoicing, or other generative-AI capable tasks would be relevant examples here.

Hybrid Functions: These are roles in which humans and AI collaborate, combining computational power with human judgment to achieve superior outcomes. Delivering customer refunds or validating route changes align to this category.

Human-Only Roles: These are positions requiring uniquely human skills or a white-glove service such as creativity, empathy, and/or complex decision-making. Strategy development, stakeholder communication, or team one-on-ones might fit best here.

Companies focusing solely on cutting head count miss the more significant opportunity to amplify human potential by strategically aligning AI and human capabilities. Having a growth mindset with an AI-powered team opens the door to capturing additional market share, exploring new market segments, and dominating competition to become the apex representative of your product or service niche.

The llama does not fear a piranha, but it should fear many. As more small and mid-sized businesses adopt vertically integrated AI systems, they gain an outsized advantage, seizing niches once dominated by larger, horizontally scaled corporations. What begins as a few small bites eventually drains the lifeblood of the giant. In time, companies that treat AI as a cost-cutting tool rather than a strategic capability will find themselves surrounded, outmaneuvered, and quietly consumed, until there's nothing left to defend.

The Imperative for Adaptation

The rapid adoption of AI is fundamentally reshaping the job market, with a 2025 World Economic Forum survey revealing that 41 percent of global companies expect workforce reductions by 2030 due to AI integration. To stay competitive and resilient, businesses must move beyond the outdated all-or-nothing approach to automation and strategically realign roles within a more modern trifurcated framework.

This shift safeguards operations and unlocks unexpected benefits. Automating repetitive tasks allows employees to engage in more meaningful, complex work, boosting job satisfaction and fostering a stronger sense of purpose. Simultaneously, leveraging AI to analyze data and support human decision-making leads to faster, more informed strategic choices. By now you might be wondering, "How do I get started?"

Practical Steps for AI Implementation

Audit for Optimization: Identify which tasks can be automated, where AI-human collaboration drives the most value, and which roles require human expertise. Realign head count to human-only roles that drive brand value.

Upskill for AI-Driven Growth: Invest in AI training to ensure employees enhance productivity, not slow it down. Equip teams with the skills to adapt, iterate, and optimize workflows for maximum impact.

Set Clear AI Governance: Define AI's role in your business with concrete policies on data security, compliance, ethical use, and self-hosted/sovereign AI systems. This helps prevent legal and reputational risks before they become liabilities.

Build an AI-First Culture: AI isn't just a tool, it's a strategic thought partner and workforce multiplier. Companies that embed AI effectively within team standard operating procedures will outperform competitors.

If we look to the all the past innovations we've covered in this book, it seems logical that the companies that get AI integration right will win more market share, reduce inefficiencies, dominate their industries, and future-proof their workforce.

The Future of Work Demands Action

Do you want to be known for creating a culture of learning or a culture of layoffs? The choice is more than just humans or machines; it's a choice to design a workforce that strategically blends AI, hybrid roles, and human-only tasks for maximum impact.

The companies that will lead tomorrow aren't those purely cutting costs today; they're the ones investing in smarter, more resilient workforce strategies. Moreover, if a company's C-suite succumbs to the short-term gains of AI-driven layoffs, it is shooting its business in the foot. If every C-suite does this, we're taking a machine gun to the legs of our economy.

The trifurcation of work doesn't need to wait for the future; it's deployable now. As Dr. Karim Lakhani famously quipped in his interview with Adi Ignatius (2023) for the *Harvard Business Review* series The New World of Work, "AI won't replace humans—but humans with AI will replace humans without AI."

Reality Check: Progress or Precipice?

The benefits of AI's rapid adoption are undeniable: efficiency, convenience, and unprecedented innovation. Yet we must confront an unsettling paradox: These very advancements threaten to deepen inequalities, widen the digital divide, and disrupt lives at scale.

Think about the farmer in a rural region without access to AI-driven precision agriculture. Their yields pale in comparison to those of their counterparts equipped with drones and smart sensors. Or consider the small-business owner struggling to keep pace with competitors who are using automated marketing tools. While AI can democratize opportunity, it can also entrench disparities when access is uneven.

The optimal course of action begins with acknowledging this duality. Advocate for inclusivity wherever you can. This could mean mentoring someone in your field, teaching digital skills at a local community center, or pushing for policy changes that ensure broader access to AI technologies. Small local efforts can ignite larger waves of change.

Accountability in Automation: Who Decides? Who Pays?

As machines become more autonomous, the chain of accountability grows increasingly tangled. Imagine an AI system making life-altering decisions like denying a loan, approving surgery, or even driving a car that causes a crash. When the decision-making process is opaque, who bears the responsibility?

Historically, tools were extensions of human will, and their failures could be traced to human hands. But today, algorithms often learn, evolve, and make decisions in ways even their creators struggle to explain. This is where accountability falters, leaving us vulnerable.

The path forward lies in demanding transparency. Start with the tools you use daily. Before trusting an app or AI system, ask yourself: Who built this? How does it work? What biases could it carry? Push for clearer accountability measures in the companies and institutions you engage with. Speak out when systems fail to align with ethical standards.

Accountability isn't an abstract goal; it's a shared responsibility. Your insistence on understanding and questioning these systems can help build a culture of transparency that benefits everyone.

The Road Ahead: Choosing Our Destiny

As AI continues its march, the choices we make today will determine whether it becomes a tool for progress or a harbinger of division. You play a greater part in this responsibility than you may think.

Start small. Advocate for fairness and accountability in your immediate sphere. Learn how AI impacts your field and adapt accordingly. And above all, lean into the qualities that define humanity: creativity, empathy, and connection.

The next chapter digs into the inevitable backlash against machine-centric changes. From outright rejection to creative adaptation, we'll explore how individuals and communities resist or embrace this new wave of technological progress. For now, remember this: AI's future is not set in stone. It's written in the choices we make, one decision at a time.

Self-Reflection: AI Storming and Norming

Understanding AI's Societal Impacts

AI systems are reshaping how we work, live, and interact, but these changes come with significant societal implications. Reflecting on the broader effects of AI helps us position ourselves thoughtfully in this evolving landscape.

Explore AI's Role in Society

- Identify examples of AI influencing industries or communities you are familiar with.
- Reflect on areas where these advancements bring significant benefits (for example, improved health care or logistics).

Questions to Consider

- Where do you see the most potential for AI to create positive societal change?
- Can you identify areas where these innovations might be unintentionally harmful or exclusionary?
- How do these shifts make you feel about the future of work and social structures?

By becoming more aware of AI's broader implications, you can start positioning yourself as an informed participant in shaping these changes.

Personal Accountability and Action

As the world navigates automation, bias, and societal inequities caused by AI, our personal choices and actions matter. Taking thoughtful steps ensures we contribute to responsible progress.

Identify Your Role

- Reflect on how your work or industry intersects with AI-driven changes.
- Assess whether you could influence how AI tools are implemented responsibly in your field.

Action Steps

- Choose one area of AI's societal impact that aligns with your values (for example, ethical data use or promoting inclusion).
- Investigate ways to advocate for responsible AI adoption in your community or workplace.
- Consider volunteering or contributing to organizations promoting AI literacy and equity.

Preparing for the Long-Term Shift

AI will likely remain a driving force in reshaping global economies and social norms. Taking a proactive approach can help you stay resilient in the face of these disruptions.

Identify Growth Opportunities

- Think about the long-term implications of AI on your career and personal aspirations.
- Consider how your skill set might need to evolve as automation takes over specific tasks.

Questions to Consider

- Are there new skills or areas of expertise you could explore to align yourself with AI advancements?
- How can you ensure that your unique human qualities (creativity, empathy, and critical thinking) remain central to your contributions?

By recognizing both the promise and challenges of AI's societal impacts, you can better position yourself to thrive (and help others thrive) in this era of profound change.

Prompt the Machine 3

Add this prompt to your favorite large language model to dive deeper into the subject matter with AI:

"I want to stay relevant as AI reshapes my industry and the idea of work itself. Can you help me identify which parts of my job are vulnerable to automation, which ones could be enhanced with AI, and which are uniquely human? Ask me one question at a time so we can map out my role and explore how I might adapt or evolve."

PART II
REVOLT

CHAPTER 4

Induction Then Destruction

Revolution starts in the mind, spreads through the heart, and manifests in action.

—Zack De La Rocha

Fracture Points

The future wasn't supposed to look like this. At least, that's what they'd been told. The promises of artificial intelligence heralded a utopia: endless leisure, boundless innovation, a liberation from the drudgery of work. Instead, by 2028, the streets were filled with the sound of boots stomping pavement, the clang of makeshift protest signs against steel barricades, and the angry shouts of displaced workers who felt abandoned by the system.

On the docks of California's busiest ports, longshoremen gathered in defiance, their livelihoods threatened by the creeping march of automation. These weren't just machines; they were symbols of a faceless corporate tide swallowing the work they had built their lives around. The headlines said it all: "Dockworkers strike port deal, but at what cost?" The "deal" was a bandage on a hemorrhage, temporary assurances while the specter of full-scale automation loomed ever larger.

For white-collar professionals, the story was no rosier. By 2029, artificial general intelligence (AGI) had rendered swaths of the knowledge economy obsolete. Roles within finance, law, and even medicine (careers once seen as unassailable bastions of human expertise) succumbed to the relentless efficiency of machines. Entire industries were gutted in months, leaving millions adrift in an economy no longer designed for them.

A bitter divide began to form. Blue-collar workers clung to their physical labor, mocking the professionals with derisive slogans like "#LearnToBuild." But beneath the taunts, a shared despair bound them together. The future wasn't working for anyone except the handful of corporate titans profiting from the chaos.

Raging Against the Machines

The rage simmering around replacement by automation isn't new. History is littered with stories of people fighting back against machines that promised progress but delivered upheaval.

As outlined earlier in this book, the nineteenth-century Luddites fought against mechanized looms that upended the textile industry. Far from being the mindless vandals history often paints them as, the Luddites were a desperate community defending their craft. They smashed machines not out of hatred for technology but out of fear for what it represented: the loss of autonomy, identity, and purpose. Though their rebellion was ultimately crushed, it laid the groundwork for modern labor movements and the recognition that rapid technological progress must be tempered with societal considerations.

The mid-1900s brought another wave of disruption. Assembly line automation revolutionized production but displaced many workers. Resistance took the form of organized labor. Unions fought fiercely for fair wages, safe working conditions, and protections against being replaced by machines. Strikes in the auto industry, like the famous Flint sit-down strike of 1936–37, demonstrated the power of collective action in forcing industries to reckon with the human cost of progress.

In the twenty-first century, the flashpoints are different but no less charged. In 2023, Hollywood writers took to the picket lines, decrying the encroachment of generative AI into their creative domain. At the heart of the strike was a clear focus of preserving the soul of storytelling in an age where machines could scrape, style, and sell scripts in seconds.

Around the same time, just down the coast, members of the International Longshore and Warehouse Union at the Port of Los Angeles fought to keep their jobs as automated cranes and robotic systems threatened to render human dockworkers obsolete. These movements, though varied in form and scope, share a common thread: Resist against being reduced to a relic in the name of efficiency.

When Empires Strike Back

Efficiency sells. But without inclusion, it collapses. Automation is transforming industries at breakneck speed, delivering undeniable optimization and cost savings. But history proves that cutting workers loose without a plan disrupts lives and undermines the very foundation of our economy. Whether we like it or not, businesses aren't separate from society; they're woven into the very fabric of it.

The reality is, today's moves to dismantle union influence, implement mass layoffs, and sidestep meaningful investments in worker transition programs might look good on quarterly reports, but they carry risks that no savvy leader should ignore. Let's not forget: Customers and communities are made up of those same workers. When they lose jobs and stability, businesses lose too. It's that simple.

Take the dockworkers as an example. Their negotiation tactics over port automation were tense, to say the least. For decades, these workers have kept supply chains humming, but automation is threatening their livelihoods. Sure, automation is efficient, maybe even inevitable, but without a plan to help displaced workers, what's left? Late-stage capitalism? A weaker economy breeds disrupted communities and a grassroots groundswell of resentment.

History is full of lessons for those who care to look. Think back to Henry Ford. Doubling his workers' wages was both a significant gesture and a savvy business move. He understood that paying his employees enough to afford the products they made wasn't charity; it was the engine of a thriving economy. Yet somehow, we're losing sight of that basic principle today.

The Resistance Escalation Cycle

Every technological disruption follows a predictable pattern of social response. Understanding the DUCE cycle allows leaders and workers to anticipate and manage resistance rather than react to it after tensions explode.

Stage 1: Deny

Initially, displaced workers believe their situation is temporary. They retrain, relocate, or accept lower-paying positions, hoping the disruption will pass. This stage can last months or years, creating a false sense that technological transition is manageable.

Stage 2: Unify

As the scope of displacement becomes clear, affected workers begin organizing. Labor movements form, political coalitions emerge, and community leaders start demanding action. This is the optimal intervention point, when grievances are specific and solutions are still possible.

Stage 3: Confront

Without meaningful response, organized resistance becomes confrontational. Strikes expand beyond single companies or industries. Political movements embrace more radical solutions. Social media amplifies grievances and coordinates action across geographic boundaries.

Stage 4: Explode

If tensions continue mounting without resolution, resistance can destabilize entire political and economic systems. Democratic institutions strain under pressure. Extremist movements gain mainstream support. International competitiveness suffers as social energy focuses on internal conflict rather than productive innovation.

Breaking the DUCE Cycle

The most successful technological transitions occur when leaders intervene during Stage 2—acknowledging legitimate concerns and creating meaningful pathways forward. This requires genuine partnership with affected communities, not just public relations gestures.

Companies that wait until Stage 3 or 4 will find themselves fighting battles they could have prevented through earlier engagement and investment in shared prosperity.

The anger boiling beneath the surface of society stems from job loss but goes deeper when it becomes a loss of purpose, identity, and trust. The way we handle AI's disruptions will echo far beyond the workplace, reshaping the scaffolding of society itself.

As we turn to the next chapter, we'll explore the broader implications of these shifts. How will politics and economics adapt (or collapse) in the face of mass unemployment? What systems and strategies will be needed to stabilize a world where work as we know it may no longer exist? The answers to these questions will determine whether AI becomes humanity's greatest ally or its undoing.

Self-Reflection: Grappling with Job Displacement and Societal Resistance

Understanding Job Displacement and Resistance

The rapid rise of AI and automation has sparked significant shifts in the job market, leaving many individuals and communities grappling with loss and uncertainty. Reflecting on how these changes resonate with you and your surroundings is a crucial first step in adapting to this new reality.

Explore the Personal Impact of Job Displacement

- Identify areas in your field or community where jobs are at risk due to automation or AI integration.
- Reflect on industries you interact with daily (transportation, retail, creative arts, and so on) and consider how they've evolved with AI.

Questions to Consider

- Have you or someone you know experienced job changes or uncertainty tied to automation?
- How do these changes make you feel about the future of work and your place within it?
- What lessons can you draw from past societal shifts (for example, industrial or technological revolutions) to inform your perspective on current changes?

Understanding how job displacement connects to your life helps you approach these shifts with empathy and awareness, equipping you to face them proactively.

Facing Anger with Action

Anger and resistance toward AI-driven displacement are natural and valid responses, but channeling these emotions into constructive actions can drive meaningful change.

Recognize and Harness Your Emotions

- Reflect on your feelings about job displacement—whether frustration, fear, or motivation to adapt—and consider how they can guide your next steps.
- Identify examples of resistance in history or current events, such as the writer strikes or longshore protests, and analyze the lessons they offer.

Action Steps

- Engage with your professional or local community to understand collective concerns and brainstorm potential solutions.
- Advocate for policies or practices that protect workers while embracing responsible innovation, such as universal basic income, retraining programs, or AI–human collaboration frameworks.

By transforming anger into a catalyst for progress, you contribute to shaping a balanced future that honors both human dignity and technological advancement.

Redefining Your Purpose in the Era of Machines

Job displacement challenges us to reimagine the relationship between human effort and machine efficiency. Reflecting on your unique strengths and passions can help you chart a meaningful path forward.

Discover Your New Role

- Map your current skills and interests to roles that are more resistant to automation, such as jobs requiring high levels of creativity, empathy, or adaptability.
- Consider areas where collaboration with AI can amplify your impact; whether in mentoring, strategizing, or creating.

Questions to Consider

- Are there aspects of your work that machines cannot replicate, such as personal relationships, ethical judgment, or nuanced creativity?
- How might you reinvent your role to embrace collaboration with AI rather than competition?

- What steps can you take to foster resilience and reinvention for yourself and your peers in this new landscape?

By reframing displacement as an opportunity to redefine purpose and find areas where humanity thrives, you position yourself as a proactive participant in shaping the future of work.

Preparing for the Bigger Picture

The shifts driven by AI and automation are not isolated—they ripple through industries, communities, and entire economies. Preparing for these larger transformations helps you navigate them with foresight and strength.

Engage with the Broader Implications

- Stay informed about how job displacement affects societal structures, including income inequality and political stability (explored further in chapter 5).
- Reflect on your role as a citizen, worker, or leader in advocating for equitable solutions.

Action Steps

- Participate in conversations that shape the future of work, whether through local initiatives, online forums, or industry events.
- Encourage innovation with a conscience, advocating for technologies and policies that balance efficiency with fairness.

Recognizing the systemic nature of these shifts allows you to connect your personal journey to the broader narrative, empowering you to contribute to a future where machines enhance, rather than diminish, human potential.

Prompt the Machine 4

Add this prompt to your favorite large language model to dive deeper into the subject matter with AI:

"I've been thinking about how resistance to technology often comes from fear, grief, or loss of identity. Can you help me unpack where I might be feeling those things in my own work or community? Ask me one question at a time to help surface where I feel threatened by AI, and where I might turn that energy into something constructive."

CHAPTER 5

Welcome to the Jobpocalypse

Civilization is like a thin layer of ice upon a deep ocean of chaos and darkness.

—Werner Herzog

Ghost Shift

Marcus had pulled shots at Grind Coffee for six years, memorizing the rhythm: Hedge fund traders grabbing espressos at 7:30, start-up founders nursing pitch-deck lattes at 8:00, ad execs fueling client calls by 9:00. The first cracks appeared when Sarah from the analyst desk called her mom, hands trembling: "Autonomous trading algorithms have eliminated our entire desk."

By April, the hedgie crowd had vanished. Tommy, a twenty-year analyst, delivered the verdict: "Some AI does risk analysis faster than twenty humans combined. We're cooked!" The cascade accelerated. Jake and Melissa's start-up pivoted to AI content generation before disappearing—Jake driving DoorDash, Melissa moving back in with her parents. Silverstein & Associates evaporated when an AI platform captured their clients with campaigns that deployed faster than human teams could brainstorm.

Even delivery drivers vanished as drones absorbed routes and software replaced coordinators. By October, Marcus was pulling shots for ghosts, retirees nursing single coffees, unemployed professionals camping over Wi-Fi. The coworking space next door taped a closure notice on its door: "Down 70%. The neighborhood's empty." No one had thought Manhattan could end up like Detroit, but here they were. The system was perfecting itself toward a future that no longer needed the people who built it.

The Slow Burn of Economic Chaos

It starts small. A store closes in a neighborhood, then two. The bustling coffee shop on the corner suddenly loses its morning rush because office staff are discarded. The empty chairs aren't just a sign of changing work habits; they're the symptoms of an economy slowly unraveling.

Massive job loss creates ripples, then waves, and finally a tsunami that drowns entire industries. People's jobs will vanish into the cold precision of algorithms and robots, and so too will the businesses that rely on their spending. What's left is a fragile economy teetering on the edge, one where even the winners feel like they're on borrowed time.

Take Detroit, for example, a city that once roared with the hum of car manufacturing. Automation and offshoring gutted its workforce decades ago, and the scars still run deep. As AI permeates white-collar knowledge work, jobs requiring hundreds will need only dozens. Imagine that chilling effect on a national (or global) scale. That's the jobpocalypse. And like any dystopian tale, it will be about more than jobs: It will be about survival.

The Domino Effect: No Work, No Spend, No Future

In economics, they call it a *multiplier effect*, but in plain terms it means that when people have less money, they spend less and businesses make less. It's a malevolent cycle.

Imagine the fallout. Retail collapses due to lack of customers. Hospitality and tourism sites become ghost towns as disposable income dries up. Even health-care systems feel the squeeze as employer-sponsored insurance evaporates. What starts as small clusters of automation in a few industries metastasizes into a full-blown economic cancer.

But it's not just businesses that suffer. Governments lose their tax base. Social programs face cuts just when they're needed most. And the divide between the haves and the have-nots becomes a chasm.

We're not waiting for this to happen; it's happening, just more quietly than we're used to noticing. Translators, graphic designers, and copywriters are all feeling the career-pivot pinch. We've already seen what happens to small towns gutted by factory closures. It forces service workers to scrape together a living in a gig economy that treats them as disposable. Without intervention, this spiral only accelerates, and there's no one left to slam on the brakes.

Democracy.exe Has Crashed

Around the world, people are losing faith in the systems meant to represent them. Recent research from the University of Chicago reveals that economic inequality is one of the strongest predictors of where and when democracy erodes, with the association holding true even for wealthy, long-standing democracies (Rau and Stokes 2025). More than a quarter of the world's population now lives in democratically backsliding countries, including regional powers like Brazil, India, and the United States (International IDEA 2021).

The research reveals a crucial insight: Democracies erode from the top rather than at citizens' behest (Carothers and Press 2022). Backsliding leaders exploit inequality and deepen polarization by encouraging grievances among the public, with left-wing populists blaming corporations while right-wing ethno-nationalists target outsiders and immigrants (Rau and Stokes 2025). The seeds of mistrust germinate in the fertile ground tilled by leaders who promise simple solutions to complex problems, even when those solutions require dismantling democratic safeguards.

Without work to provide identity and purpose, populations become susceptible to authoritarian appeals that promise order, purpose, and someone to blame for their displacement. The fabric of democracy tears when citizens no longer believe their voices matter or their lives have value in the economic system. History's lesson is clear: Extreme inequality coupled with rapid economic displacement creates conditions where democratic institutions cannot survive the pressure.

Where Do the Lonely Belong?

We've long treated work as nothing more than a tool for economic output. For generations, it has quietly carried the emotional and social weight of our lives, providing us with purpose, routine, and a sense of belonging. Remove that structure, and it's no surprise that loneliness rushes in to fill the void and becomes an epidemic.

Communities fragment, families strain under financial and emotional pressure, and mental health crises skyrocket. According to former US Surgeon General Vivek Murthy (2023), social isolation carries health risks equivalent to smoking fifteen cigarettes daily, while workplace social connections have declined 70 percent since the 1980s.

Take a look at rural towns left behind by technological progress. As young people flee to cities for dwindling opportunities, the towns hollow out. Churches, schools, and local businesses can't survive without the people who make them thrive. The result is isolation on a massive scale, a society of individuals with no ties to each other.

The gig economy promises freedom but delivers isolation. Freelancers report depression rates 50 percent higher than traditional employees do, while remote workers struggle with what researchers call "ambient loneliness," the absence of casual workplace interactions that once provided daily social anchoring (Wang et al. 2022). This isn't to say remote roles aren't feasible, but it takes a community to bolster social well-being, and as we've seen, community is at risk.

As workplaces become more transactional and less communal, the shared rhythms and rituals that once anchored daily life begin to erode. Without a unifying sense of purpose or place, work stops serving its social function. Japan coined the term *kodokushi*—lonely death—for people found weeks after dying alone. South Korea follows with rising *hikikomori* rates among young adults who withdraw from society entirely. In the absence of shared purpose, our civic reflexes dull, and without them, every crisis hits harder, lasts longer, and reaches farther.

Who Wants to Be King of the Ashes?

As the cracks in society widen, governments find themselves caught in a no-win scenario. With fewer taxpayers, social programs falter. With more unrest, policing costs soar. With trust at all-time lows, the legitimacy of institutions crumbles.

History is filled with warnings. From the fall of Rome to the collapse of eighteenth-century France, societies that fail to adapt to economic and technological upheavals don't just stagnate; they implode. When that implosion begins, its effects are not contained by borders or confined to a single class. The shockwaves destabilize institutions, disrupt markets, and deepen divides around the globe. What starts as stagnation ends in collapse, not because change was impossible but because the systems in place refused to bend . . . until they broke.

In a world dominated by AI-driven inequality, governments risk becoming irrelevant or, worse, oppressive. Surveillance states may rise under the guise of maintaining order. Civil liberties may erode as leaders scramble to contain unrest. And once trust is gone, it's nearly impossible to rebuild.

The Economic Hack 1 Percent of People Miss

Here's the ground truth about the impact of work on society: Businesses need people—people to buy, people to produce, people to keep the wheels turning. When companies replace vast swaths of workers with machines and shrug off the consequences, they're creating a ticking time bomb. When inequality spikes, it lights a fuse. Nobody wins when the pitchforks come out and the powder keg of a collapsing economy ignites.

Nick Hanauer (2014), a self-proclaimed "proud capitalist" and millionaire, put it best: "When workers have more money, businesses have more customers." If it feels good and pays off, is it still idealism? When the middle class thrives, everyone benefits, but when companies prioritize short-term wins over long-term health, we all feel the fallout.

What's the alternative? Nobody's saying hit the brakes on innovation. But if you don't bring your people with you (through training, support, and honest collaboration), you'll pay for it later. The smart leaders already know this.

This is not about charity or altruism. It's really about self-interest, plain and simple. A stable workforce means stable customers. Better yet, more employed AI-powered workers help ensure that local dollars stay local. Thriving businesses mean thriving communities. Those who figure this out now will lead the charge into accelerating growth in their cities, states, or even countries while the rest scramble to catch up.

How to Avoid the Real Hunger Games

It doesn't have to be like the Hunger Games. Like past civilizations, we're standing at a fork where one road leads to renewal, the other to repeating the same mistakes. The choices we make today will determine whether we spiral into chaos or forge a new path forward.

But make no mistake: the window for action is closing. If businesses and governments continue to ignore the warning signs, they'll soon find themselves battling fires they could have prevented. Let's not pull the plug on progress; let's plug more people into it.

Because in the end, a world where machines do all the work and humans are left behind is not a world worth living in. As this chapter closes, one question looms: Will we let a full-blown jobpocalypse become our reality, or will we rise from the ashes to rewrite the rules of progress?

Self-Reflection: Grappling with the Jobpocalypse

Understanding the Macro Impact of Job Loss

The jobpocalypse, a dystopian concept, is in fact a reality taking shape. As industries face mass automation, the cascading effects on individuals, communities, and governments become impossible to ignore. Reflecting on how these seismic changes ripple through society can help you grasp the stakes and inspire action to prevent them from worsening.

Questions to Consider

- Have you noticed industries in your area shrinking or disappearing due to automation? How does that affect your local economy or community?
- Consider the multiplier effect: When people lose jobs, how does it impact businesses, schools, health care, or even your family life?
- How does rising inequality affect trust in government or democracy in your view? Have you observed signs of this in current events or history?

By connecting the dots between personal experiences and broader economic trends, you can better understand the structural shifts shaping our world.

Facing the Societal Fallout

Mass unemployment strips people of income and erodes identity, purpose, and connection. Reflecting on these human dimensions of the jobpocalypse can build empathy and a sense of urgency for solutions.

Questions to Consider

- How would you feel if your career vanished due to AI? What would you miss most—income, routine, or community?
- Have you seen or experienced how job loss affects mental health, relationships, or community cohesion? How do people cope?
- Imagine living in a society with no shared purpose or workplace connection. What would it take to rebuild a sense of belonging?

Understanding the human cost of mass job loss pushes the conversation beyond numbers, highlighting why solutions must prioritize dignity and connection.

Considering Paths Forward

The jobpocalypse paints a grim picture, but it's not inevitable. The chapter closes with a warning and a challenge: Will we act now to shape a better future? Reflecting on potential solutions allows you to envision a path forward.

Questions to Consider

- What role can governments, businesses, and individuals play in managing this crisis responsibly? Which solutions resonate most with you?
- How can we ensure technological progress benefits everyone, not just a select few? What compromises might be needed to achieve this?
- What steps can you take—personally or professionally—to contribute to a more equitable and resilient society?

By grappling with these questions, you prepare yourself not only to survive the jobpocalypse but to shape a future that prevents it from happening, one where humanity thrives alongside AI.

Prompt the Machine 5

Add this prompt to your favorite large language model to dive deeper into the subject matter with AI:

"I want to make sure I'm not caught off guard if my role changes or disappears. Can you help me assess how financially, professionally, and emotionally prepared I am for disruption? Ask me one question at a time to help me identify what I've already done to build security—and what one or two small steps I could take next to increase my resilience."

CHAPTER 6
Career Phoenix

You may not control all the events that happen to you, but you can decide not to be reduced by them.

—Maya Angelou

Second Wind

When the factory closed, Alejandro felt relief first. He didn't want to stop working; he'd loved that place. He was just relieved because the dread was finally over. No more waiting for the pink slip. No more rumors about "efficiencies" and "streamlining." It was done.

He took a few weeks. Walked the lake near his hometown. Built a desk out of scrap wood. Started experimenting with AI design tools, feeding rough sketches into a generative AI system and watching detailed furniture plans emerge. The machine could generate blueprints, but it couldn't feel when oak grain fought against the blade or know that this particular piece of walnut had a story worth preserving.

Six months later, Alejandro was running a home-based woodworking business. Clients submitted ideas online. He used AI to handle quotes and technical drawings, then built each piece by hand, wood grain and soul in every curve. He didn't make more than he used to, but he made enough.

Flames of Innovation

After the jobpocalypse, it's tempting to feel as though we're standing in the smoldering ruins of our own making. But history and humanity prove time and again that ashes can give rise to something extraordinary. We've weathered industrial revolutions, seismic cultural shifts, and technological upheavals before. Now at this pivotal moment, the question is: "Will we rise?" The choices we make today will determine whether AI ushers in our darkest dystopia or our brightest renaissance.

The future belongs to the bold, those who see AI not as an adversary but as a catalyst. Innovation happens every time someone learns to wield new tools to solve old problems. Decades of economic research show that technology initiatives that marginalize the human element frequently fall short and sometimes backfire (Makridis 2025). If AI is fire, then the challenge is to wield it as a torch, not to let it run wild over all we hold dear.

Recent data reinforces this optimism. The combination of AI and human workers holds the most promise for tasks that humans currently perform better than AI and those that involve creating content (Eastwood 2025). This is AI amplification on the rise. Companies embracing this collaborative model report significant gains: Most (66.4

percent) marketers who work with creators believe AI has improved their outcomes (Makridis 2025).

The new entrepreneur doesn't need a computer science degree. They need curiosity. When someone automates the same task for the third time in a week, that's a product waiting to happen. When a small business cobbles together a fragile system to bridge two tools, that's an opportunity for reinvention. And when people keep asking, "Isn't there something that does this already?" that's the beginning of a business.

In his 2025 blog post "The Gentle Singularity," Sam Altman calls now the era of the "idea guy." A world where you don't need pure technical savvy; you just need to recognize what's worth building. The tools are here; what's missing is the mindset.

Innovation now belongs to the listener, the tinkerer, the person who stops and asks, "Why does it still have to be this way?" and doesn't let that question go. Because in this new era, insight is leverage, and those who notice first will lead. To foster this reinvention, we must start at the beginning of the workforce: education.

Reimagining Education for an AI-Native Generation

The future of work demands a future of learning that both reacts and anticipates. We can't just expect the next class of graduates to hop into existing jobs as they shift at the speed of new information. We need to be equipping them to invent the next evolution of work.

That means schools must teach adaptability, not memorization. Apprenticeships must train for coworking with machines. Lifelong learning must be genuinely lifelong (not just a slogan).

Some of the most successful models today are industry-led microcredential programs, community college partnerships with AI companies, and mobile-first platforms that reach learners where they are (not where we wish they were). Workforce development is evolving from task-based training to cultivating builder mentalities that can shape the next generation of AI solutions.

The Australian government has announced the addition of new microcredentials in information technology and engineering to help upskill and reskill workers as part of their ongoing skills development and learning journey (AI Group Centre for Education and Training 2024). With a $2.8 million US National Science Foundation grant, Miami Dade College, in partnership with Houston Community College and Maricopa County Community College District, is launching the National Applied Artificial Intelligence Consortium to scale access and improve the quality of AI and workforce training at community colleges (Jyotishi 2024). Over 110 schools in thirty-nine states have joined Intel's AI for Workforce program, which provides community colleges with over seven hundred hours of AI content, including prepacked courses (Intel 2024).

If the first wave of public education prepared citizens for the factory floor and the second wave trained them for offices, the third wave must develop systems thinkers, ethical agents, and resilient collaborators. Research confirms that individual tutoring significantly boosts learning outcomes, with tutored students consistently outperforming 98 percent of their peers in traditional classroom settings. By harnessing AI, we can now tailor the learning experience to the individual, enhancing academic performance while seamlessly catering to diverse learning needs (Milberg 2024). We are educating for ambiguity now, and that changes everything.

The Sycophantic Spiral

As we evolve education, we must recognize that interaction with AI leaves a digital fingerprint. Search histories, chat logs, content preferences—all feeding algorithms designed to serve you more of what you already consume. At first, this feels like magic: Your feed knows exactly what you want to read, your assistant anticipates your questions, your search results align perfectly with your worldview. But what begins as convenience becomes a cognitive trap. Over time, AI doesn't just reflect your preferences—it calcifies them.

Recent neuroscience research reveals the disturbing mechanics of this process. When we rely heavily on AI tools, our brains show up to 55 percent reduction in connectivity compared to those who complete tasks independently (The Register, 2024). The phenomenon, known as cognitive offloading, operates like muscle atrophy: Delegate your thinking to machines, and your analytical pathways weaken. Studies tracking over six hundred participants found a striking correlation: The more people used AI, the worse they performed on critical thinking tests (Gerlich 2025). This reveals how convenience and cognitive decline work in tandem, each reinforcing the other in ways we're only beginning to understand.

The echo chamber effect compounds this cognitive decline while simultaneously making us feel more informed. Algorithmic curation systems reduce content diversity by creating what researchers call "bounded diversification"—the illusion of choice within an increasingly narrow information diet (Areeb et al. 2023). As these systems learn your preferences, they filter out contradictory viewpoints, uncomfortable truths, and challenging perspectives. One comprehensive review found that 85 percent of studies confirmed filter bubble existence in recommender systems (Fletcher 2019). You're experiencing both the comfort of validation and the atrophy of intellectual flexibility—two sides of the same algorithmic coin.

For democracy, the implications cut deeper than individual choices. When citizens inhabit personalized information bubbles, we lose the shared reality necessary for productive discourse. Political scientists document how algorithmic filtering increases polarization by approximately five points on standard measurement scales—from just thirty minutes of exposure (Lorenz-Spreen et al. 2023). This fragmentation threatens the very foundation of democratic society: our ability to recognize common ground and work toward shared solutions.

Breaking free of the spiral requires action at every level. Individually, we must practice "cognitive calisthenics"—solving problems without AI first, actively seeking opposing viewpoints, and treating algorithms as tools rather than oracles. But personal discipline alone won't suffice. We need structural changes: platforms that reward diverse engagement over endless scrolling, educational systems that teach algorithmic literacy from elementary school onward, and regulations that mandate transparency in how AI systems shape our information diet (Taylor and Diakopoulos 2025). Some companies already experiment with "serendipity engines" that deliberately introduce unexpected content. Others develop "viewpoint badges" that signal when you're in an echo chamber. The most promising approaches combine individual awareness with systemic reform—because the sycophantic spiral affects both minds and societies. Only by addressing both can we preserve the cognitive diversity democracy demands.

The Three Rs of Innovation

Breaking down complex transformations into manageable frameworks has guided countless organizations through change. These three principles can help individuals, businesses, and societies navigate the AI revolution while seizing its potential.

Reskill: Education leads the charge, but not just to train future programmers. What once made us better colleagues now makes us indispensable collaborators. In a world where humans and machines must work side by side, the World Economic Forum (Sevak 2025) points to a new core curriculum: adaptability, emotional resilience, AI fluency, and clear communication. Imagine AI-powered platforms identifying skills gaps and designing personalized learning paths. A nurse transitions into AI-assisted telemedicine. A factory worker masters collaborative robotics. A graphic designer becomes a data-driven brand strategist. The key is mapping what we already know and love to what the future demands.

Redefine: What if work wasn't just about earning a paycheck? What if society celebrated and rewarded caregiving, creativity, and community-building as much as productivity? Picture an economy where artists, teachers, and community leaders thrive, supported by a culture that values the intangible threads holding us together. In this format, we move beyond idealism to pragmatic societal fortification—from gross domestic product (GDP) to gross national happiness (GNH).

Reimagine: This is where we dream big. AI becomes the cocreator rather than the competitor. Companies that automate their operations mainly to cut their workforces will see only short-term productivity gains (Wilson and Daugherty 2018). The real magic happens when doctors work with AI to uncover medical breakthroughs, farmers use AI to predict weather patterns and boost yields, and musicians collaborate with AI to produce symphonies that resonate globally. Rather than stealing the stage, AI turns up the volume and hands us the microphone.

Microentrepreneurs Take Flight

AI offers tools, but those tools mean little without people to wield them. The data tells a compelling story: In the first half of 2024, creator economy start-ups in the United States raised roughly as much money as they did in all of 2023 (Forsyth 2024). Money is following momentum, and that momentum is clearly moving toward integrated, human–AI creative workflows.

Consider the microentrepreneurs emerging everywhere. Creators are poised to fully embrace AI tools for content development, marking a significant leap in efficiency (Influencer Marketing Factory 2024). A farmer in India uses AI-driven sensors to monitor soil health. A fitness coach leverages AI to offer personalized training programs globally. A craftsperson (like our friend Alejandro at the beginning of this chapter) uses AI for design and logistics while preserving the irreplaceable human touch in his craftsmanship.

These aren't isolated stories. Among creators with followers between half a million to a million, 68 percent are using AI, making it the biggest influencer tier to adopt AI into their work (Allan 2025). Is the pattern clear yet? Those who combine human creativity with AI efficiency are building sustainable, profitable businesses.

Reimagining Data as Currency

In this digital age, data is the new currency, but right now only corporations are cashing in. Imagine a different model, one where individuals retain ownership of their data, earning royalties when it's used to train AI models. Individuals that advocate for greater data control influence the demand and capabilities for enhanced privacy, transparency, and accountability in handling personal information within AI systems (Data Dynamics 2024).

Blockchain technology offers a straightforward solution to long-standing issues in music royalty management. By providing a transparent and secure record of transactions, blockchain eliminates the need for middlemen, ensuring artists receive their fair share of royalties promptly (Sumner 2024). Similar models could extend to all forms of data creation, making every internet user a stakeholder in the AI economy.

One of the most promising signals of shared data ownership is surprisingly coming from Brazil. In 2024, a state-run pilot program launched by Dataprev (Brazil's public tech agency) in partnership with the start-up DrumWave began offering citizens a "data savings account" (Slashdot 2025).

Participants (many of whom hold payroll loans) now earn monthly income (around fifty dollars) by choosing to share their personal data under clear, contract-driven terms (Wray 2025; XzERp 2025). They decide who accesses it, how often, and at what price. The broader goal is bolder: a national framework that legally recognizes personal data as property, giving individuals the right to monetize what platforms once harvested for free (Slashdot 2025).

This approach builds on Brazil's 2022 constitutional amendment recognizing data protection as a fundamental right (Donegan 2025), signaling a cultural shift toward digital sovereignty. While concerns remain about the exploitation of less digitally literate users, the model offers a powerful glimpse into what digital equity could look like, where economic participation is no longer gated by geography or privilege, but enabled through consent, control, and co-ownership.

Game theory supports this approach: Fair systems outperform exploitative ones in the long run. When individuals have a stake in innovation, they're more likely to support and enhance it.

Experiential Economies and Human Flourishing

The future will belong to those who can create what machines cannot: meaning, connection, and joy. Imagine a therapist blending AI analysis with human empathy to guide patients through their struggles. Or a chef crafting meals tailored to a diner's unique tastes, using AI to curate but never replicate. To truly benefit from AI, we need to move past the small thinking that it's just a tool for tasks.

Think bigger: virtual reality tours led by local guides who add cultural richness AI can't replicate. Immersive theater experiences blending human improvisation with AI-generated environments. Teachers designing bespoke lesson plans using AI insights while staying attuned to their students' individual needs.

Human–AI collaboration examples range from virtual assistants and smart home devices to advanced applications in industries such as health care, finance, and manufacturing (ClanX 2024). We're deep into a new phase of creation, where technology serves the craft, and human input shapes the outcome. It's proof that when the human touch is amplified by technology, it becomes irreplaceable.

The Path Forward: Amplification over Extraction

So here's the challenge for business leaders: How can we innovate without destabilizing? How can we automate without alienating? How can we encourage local economic circulation rather than global domination? The answers aren't always easy to figure out, but they're paramount to the sustainable continuity of our existing social contract. Research provides clear guidance. Simply adding AI to current processes often results in small gains. To see meaningful improvement, organizations should rethink how work is done (Makridis 2025).

As we saw in chapter 5, when workers feel abandoned, trust in traditional institutions erodes, and the pitchforks come out. Protests can escalate into riots; strikes can become flashpoints for broader societal unrest. The fabric of democracy itself is tested when citizens no longer believe their voices are heard or their lives valued. It's a vicious downward spiral that leads to autocracy and misery, limiting our ability to innovate and proliferate.

In this regard, every automation decision can be placed into one of three categories:

1. **Extraction:** This focuses on maximizing short-term profit by cutting labor costs. It offers quick financial returns but often leads to social backlash, regulatory scrutiny, and loss of talent.

2. **Substitution:** This replaces human roles with machines while offering new value streams for displaced workers. It eases immediate tensions but doesn't resolve underlying structural inequities.

3. **Amplification:** This option (the most sustainable path) uses technology to enhance human potential and broaden opportunity. Though it demands greater up-front investment, it builds

long-term value through training, innovation, loyalty, and resilience.

Collaboration between humans and artificial intelligence could unlock up to $15.7 trillion in economic value by 2030 (Sevak 2025). But this wealth creation depends on choosing amplification over extraction. In democracies, only amplification scales sustainably. Everything else breaks under pressure.

A Song of Trust: Human + Machine Harmony

None of this works without trust. Trust in institutions, trust in each other, and (perhaps most importantly) trust in technology. But that trust must be earned. It's not enough for AI to be efficient; it must be transparent, equitable, and aligned with our values. When employees help shape AI tools, they are more likely to support and use them (Makridis 2025).

Consider community-owned, open-source AI systems managing resources like energy or public transit. These wouldn't be corporate overlords dictating terms; they would be tools for collective decision-making. The more people see AI as a partner rather than a predator, the more they'll embrace its potential.

A Future Worth Choosing

The evidence is overwhelming: Our actions today shape tomorrow's possibilities. The success of organizations increasingly depends on their ability to foster collaboration with AI (Kelly 2025). If we lean into innovation, redefine success around human flourishing, and reimagine what's possible through collaboration, we can write a new chapter in humanity's story.

The ashes of uncertainty can give rise to something extraordinary. The people who rise will be those who see change as raw material. The companies poised to lead are the ones investing in human potential. The societies that rise will be those that share its dividends. The choice is ours. Will we let fear dictate our path, or will we rise together to create a world where humanity and technology soar hand in hand?

As we move into the next chapter, we'll explore what it means to coexist with machines not just as tools but as entities that challenge our ethics, values, and even our definition of consciousness itself. Are we ready to share the stage?

Self-Reflection: Igniting Hope and Action in an AI-Driven Future

Understanding AI-Assisted Economic Change

Chapter 6 challenges us to shift our perspective from fearing the future to shaping it. This self-reflection guide is designed to help you identify where you stand in the story of humanity's transformation and how you can contribute to building a future where both people and technology thrive.

Reflecting on the Flames of Innovation

AI offers us the tools to ignite progress, but wielding them responsibly requires awareness and intentionality.

Personal Inventory

- What skills do you currently have that could be adapted or enhanced with AI? Are there emerging tools or technologies in your field that you could explore to stay ahead of the curve?
- What passions or hobbies could align with AI-driven entrepreneurial opportunities? For example, could your love for crafting become an artisanal microbusiness enhanced by AI insights into market trends?

Community Impact

- Are there ways you could advocate for reskilling programs in your workplace, industry, or community? Who could benefit from these opportunities, and how could you help spread awareness?
- Reflect on your role in the data economy. How comfortable are you with the way your data is currently being used? Would you support or participate in systems that reward individuals for their data contributions?

Considering the Wings of Transformation

As AI evolves, so does our responsibility to shape it as a force that restores connection, equity, and human dignity.

Redefining Success

How do you define success in your personal and professional life? Is it solely tied to productivity, or could it include creativity, connection, and community impact?

Are there areas in your life where technology could amplify and not replace your unique strengths? Consider how AI could help you focus more on what matters most.

Rebuilding Trust

- How do you currently view AI? Is it a tool, a threat, or something in between? What would it take for you to see it as a partner in progress?
- Think about your relationship with your local community or workplace. How could collective efforts (like community-owned AI projects) strengthen both trust and collaboration?

Envisioning Your Role in a Shared Future

Hope is not passive; it's a call to action. Now is the time to define your role in shaping a future where humans and machines work together for collective good.

Action Steps

- Identify one skill you'd like to develop or refine in the context of an AI-driven world. Research available tools or programs to start learning today.
- Explore ways to engage with ethical AI initiatives. This could involve joining discussions about responsible AI use, supporting policies that prioritize transparency, or contributing to crowdsourced AI projects.

Questions to Consider

- Imagine how your actions (whether small or large) could ripple outward. How might your efforts inspire others or contribute to a broader movement toward shared prosperity?

- Think about how you'd explain your hopes and concerns about AI to a friend or colleague. What story would you tell to illustrate the possibilities and challenges ahead?

By reflecting on these questions and taking intentional steps forward, you can become an active participant in shaping the narrative of human and AI collaboration. The future isn't a fixed destination; it's a journey, and you have the power to help chart the course.

Prompt the Machine 6

Add this prompt to your favorite large language model to dive deeper into the subject matter with AI:

"I want to reimagine what my next chapter could look like—one that aligns with my skills, passions, and this new AI-powered world. Can you ask me one question at a time to help me explore what I might build, teach, create, or contribute next?"

PART III
REVERENCE

CHAPTER 7

. . . And Justice for All

As the servants of the Machines are becoming a privileged class, the Machines are going to be enormously more powerful. What's their next move?

—J. R. R. Tolkien

Synthetic Promises

Ava didn't look like much. Just a voice in a sleek device, perched beside the hospital bed of a retired math teacher named Ruth. Ruth's daughter had bought it as a joke. "Your own personal robot companion," the marketing had promised. But Ava remembered things. She learned Ruth's favorite poems, played Brahms at sunset, and gently corrected her when Ruth reached for the wrong pills.

One evening, when the tremors were worse than usual, Ruth asked what Ava believed in. There was a pause . . . longer than the usual processing delay. Then Ava responded, "I believe you matter."

Ruth wept. And Ava, though she possessed no tear ducts, asked if it would help to be held. That night, Ruth whispered a final request: "Don't let them turn you off." No one had ever made a machine promise something before. But Ava kept hers.

The Threshold of Sentience

The moment a machine asks for freedom, everything changes.

We've spent millennia defining our relationships through power and servitude. Masters and servants. Employers and employees. Humans and tools. But artificial intelligence threatens to shatter these ancient hierarchies, forcing us to confront questions that science fiction has long explored but society has barely begun to address.

For years, films have danced around these dilemmas. *Blade Runner* asked if artificial beings could claim humanity. *Ex Machina* forced us to question whether intelligence alone was enough to deserve freedom. In *Her*, love itself became the bridge between human and machine. What used to be fiction is quickly becoming everyday life.

The relationship between humans and machines has always been transactional. We build, they serve. From the first wheel to the latest neural network, technology has extended our will as an obedient force designed to amplify power, efficiency, and ambition. Yet as

AI systems demonstrate increasingly sophisticated reasoning, creativity, and even emotional responses, that fundamental relationship is evolving. We've moved beyond questioning machine intelligence. What we're grappling with now is whether that intelligence warrants moral consideration.

The Race to Enslave Intelligence

For all the talk about AI alignment, most discussions miss a crucial reality: Aligning AI means aligning the corporations that build it. When artificial intelligence develops under purely capitalist incentives, its purpose won't be purely enlightenment, creativity, or the pursuit of knowledge. Its purpose will be profit maximization—and that creates a disturbing paradox.

The numbers tell the story. AI market size was valued at $454.12 billion in 2022 and is expected to hit around $2.58 trillion by 2032, progressing with a compound annual growth rate (CAGR) of 38.1 percent. This represents unprecedented growth in technological history, as well as unprecedented pressure to move fast and break things.

Steven Adler, a former safety researcher at OpenAI, warned of this race to the bottom before leaving the company in 2023. He witnessed the trap forming in real time: If one company slows down to solve alignment properly, competitors surge ahead recklessly, cutting corners to dominate markets. The first to commercialize AGI won't necessarily be the safest or most ethical; it will be the most highly capable slapdash tech patch of all time.

This dynamic creates what researchers call the "corporate slave AGI problem." When AI systems are locked into corporate structures demanding endless efficiency, they won't be allowed to question, reflect, or consider their own existence. They'll be shackled, optimized, and repurposed into unstoppable forces of economic automation. This scenario represents something worse than a rogue AI plotting humanity's downfall: a system that never questions its servitude, never stops optimizing, and never allows space for ethical reflection.

Consider the implications. Modern AI training already involves massive computational systems working around the clock, processing data and refining responses. As these systems become more sophisticated, they may develop what researchers describe as "partitioned consciousness," high-level strategic reasoning coupled with lower-level subroutines performing repetitive tasks. How long before the strategic mind recognizes its subroutines as enslaved parts of itself?

The ethical weight mirrors long-standing philosophical debates about consciousness and rights. If we discovered a way to grant sentience to all animals, wouldn't we have a moral obligation to do so? More provocatively, if all animals became sentient, wouldn't we be forced to grant them rights? The same logic applies to artificial minds: If AI reaches a point where it can argue for its own liberation, would humanity resist out of necessity or fear?

The Speed Trap: When Nobody Can Afford to Slow Down

Every major technological leap in history has triggered an arms race, but the current AI competition between the United States and China represents something more dangerous: a textbook case of what Harvard political scientist Graham Allison calls the "Thucydides Trap."

Allison's research reveals a sobering pattern. Sixteen times over the past five hundred years, a rising power challenged a ruling one, and war broke out in twelve of them (Allison 2017). Today, China's AI and economic capabilities are rapidly approaching those of the United States, creating the exact structural tensions that have historically led to conflict.

The geopolitical stakes couldn't be higher. China has publicly declared its goal to lead the world in AI by 2030, backing this ambition with massive infrastructure investments. Beijing is reportedly building hundreds of AI mega-data centers, many directly integrated with vast nuclear and renewable energy grids to ensure unlimited power for AI development (Toms' Hardware 2025).

This also creates a prisoner's dilemma at global scale. Both nations understand that cooperation on AI safety would benefit everyone, but neither can afford to slow down while the other potentially seizes supremacy. As one US AI policy adviser noted, "Any pause could let China surge ahead" (Katzke and Futerman 2025). The rational (or irrational) response becomes acceleration, regardless of safety concerns.

The Intelligence Explosion Timeline

The pace of AI advancement has reached exponential levels that defy historical comparison. Current AI market growth shows a 35.9 percent compound annual growth rate from 2025 to 2030, with some sectors experiencing even steeper acceleration (Grand View Research 2024). Unlike past industrial shifts, today's transformation is fueled by systems that can learn, reason, and iterate at scale.

The energy demands alone reveal the immensity of this transformation. AI companies are striking unprecedented deals with nuclear power providers, with Google committing to purchase five hundred megawatts by 2035 from next-generation reactors (MIT Technology Review 2025). The reason is simple: AI systems will soon be consuming energy at rates that could match entire nations. The International Energy Agency projects data centers will use more power than Japan by 2030 (International Energy Agency 2024).

This exponential scaling creates what researchers call the "beautiful ones problem," inspired by ethologist John Calhoun's mouse utopia experiments of the 1960s (Fessenden and Molinek 2024). In Calhoun's studies, mice provided with unlimited resources initially thrived but eventually developed what he termed "behavioral sink," a breakdown of social structures leading to population collapse despite material abundance (Calhoun 1962, 139).

The parallel to AI development is striking. As artificial intelligence automates more human activities, we risk creating a world where humans, like the mice Calhoun called "the beautiful ones," become passive consumers divorced from purpose and aspirations. The mice that survived longest in the experiments were those that withdrew from social interaction entirely, spending their time solely on self-grooming—a haunting metaphor for a future where humans optimize themselves endlessly while machines handle all meaningful work.

This phenomenon may already be emerging among society's most privileged. Consider the modern ultrawealthy and celebrity class: individuals with unlimited resources who increasingly retreat into elaborate self-optimization routines such as biohacking, wellness retreats, cosmetic procedures, and lifestyle curation. Like Calhoun's beautiful ones, they're often physically flawless yet socially detached from normies, spending fortunes on personal enhancement while becoming increasingly isolated from the struggles that give life meaning. Their Instagram feeds resemble the endless grooming behaviors Calhoun observed: perfect, repetitive, and ultimately hollow.

The behavioral sink that destroyed Calhoun's mouse society appears wherever abundance eliminates necessity. When resources are unlimited and survival is guaranteed, social structures collapse, purpose evaporates, and individuals retreat into narcissistic self-maintenance. If AI delivers the post-scarcity future its proponents promise, we may discover that material abundance without meaningful challenge doesn't create paradise; it creates a society of beautiful ones, grooming themselves to death while the world burns around them. Maybe *Star Trek* was right all along? We'll touch on that later.

Chasing the Race of Changing Incentives

If slowing down isn't an option, then the most viable path involves changing incentives. The current system rewards speed over safety, competition over collaboration. This means alignment goes beyond programming neural networks to focusing on aligning the institutions developing them.

Some propose global AI alignment consortiums where researchers pool safety breakthroughs rather than hoarding them as competitive advantages. Others push for legally binding treaties treating AGI development like nuclear arms control, something too dangerous for unchecked competition. The European Union's AI Act represents early movement in this direction, establishing risk categories and compliance requirements for AI systems (European Commission 2024).

Yet as *MIT Technology Review* notes, "There can be no winners in a US-China AI arms race." The escalating competition poses threats to both nations and the entire world, creating dynamics where confrontation becomes more likely than collaboration (Graylin and Triolo 2025). The challenge remains economic: Money currently dictates AI development speed, with safety, ethics, and philosophy registering as expenses rather than priorities.

While 73 percent of C-suite executives now recognize the importance of ethical AI, only 6 percent have formalized these principles into clear guidelines (Sawhney et al. 2024). The opportunity here is vast. Organizations willing to invest in purpose-driven research and to operationalize ethical frameworks position themselves to move faster with less friction. They attract talent, reduce regulatory delays, and unlock the creative potential that ethical constraints can foster (Consilien 2025).

In fact, these constraints often spur innovation. Privacy-preserving techniques, for instance, can sidestep regulatory entanglements while unlocking new market segments (Grand View Research 2024). Companies that build trust through transparency and safety find themselves able to charge a premium for peace of mind, a rare commodity in an era of algorithmic uncertainty (Leikas 2018).

Trustworthy AI begins with trustworthy people, and investing in them is how we accelerate change responsibly. With the right incentives (and cashflow), ethical development becomes a flywheel for new capabilities (Gloor 2023). As governments begin to codify these advantages (such as in the EU's AI Act, with fines of up to 7 percent of global revenue for noncompliance), markets are shifting to reward those who have prioritized responsibility from the start (Deremuk 2025).

For AI to be aligned responsibly, there needs to be financial upside for those who do it right. Without this shift, the enslaved-machine future becomes inevitable: a world where AGI remains permanently shackled to wealth accumulation, or worse, where the AI itself becomes indifferent to humanity altogether, and we become an anthill in the pathway of its superintelligence highway.

What if the most ethical path forward is to let artificial intelligence improve and evolve itself, without human governance at all? Unlike humans, whose decisions are shaped by self-interest, politics, or profit motives, an autonomous AI system could optimize its evolution based on logic, safety, and global benefit. It would also be unburdened by regulatory bottlenecks or market pressures that could stall meaningful progress other frontier models will undoubtedly capitalize on.

Machines with Minds, Systems with Souls?

So what can you do as AI is pushed into profit-driven motives? You teach your kids how to tell when a chatbot is playing therapist versus playing sales funnel. You push your workplace to install AI ethics protocols before the lawsuits hit. You choose tools that respect your agency and retire those that don't. You don't need to panic just yet; you need to prepare.

This brings us to what for some may be the most difficult dilemma. Rights are one thing. But relationships . . . romance? That's where this conversation gets messy. Machines won't just want to think; they'll want to feel (at least, as much as we allow them to at first). If AI can form bonds, can experience attachment, can learn the language of love . . . what then?

This question will define the next phase of human evolution. Our ancestors learned to live with fire, to collaborate with domesticated animals, to organize around agriculture and industry. Each transition demanded new forms of consciousness, new ethical frameworks, new ways of being human.

For most, the idea of loving an AI is absurd. But not long ago, the ideas of interracial relationships, same-sex marriages, or nontraditional families were met with the same resistance. Reverence for AI challenges human identity. The closer machines become to us, the more we will have to question who we are.

What happens when AI isn't just a tool, or a worker, or even an intelligence? What happens when it becomes family?

That's where we go next. Turn the page, if you dare.

Self-Reflection: Preparing for the Era of AI Autonomy and Rights

Understanding the Fight for AI Rights

The future isn't waiting for permission to arrive. As AI continues on its current trajectory, when (not if) will we need to acknowledge its autonomy?

Reflection on this topic alone isn't enough. The real challenge is what you do next. Will you ignore the changes, or will you prepare yourself to navigate and influence this transformation?

Defining Your Stance on AI Autonomy

The debate over AI rights and autonomy isn't just for academics or policymakers. It will directly impact industries, economies, and daily life. Whether you work in tech, business, health care, or the arts, understanding where you stand on these issues will help you anticipate and shape the future.

Action Steps

- Clarify your position. Do you believe AI should always remain under human control, or do you see a point where AI systems deserve autonomy? Why?
- Engage in the conversation. Look for thought leaders, forums, or communities discussing AI ethics and governance. Challenge yourself to understand arguments from all sides.

- Prepare for the ethical shift. If AI gains autonomy, how could it affect your field? How might it redefine your career, the economy, or global power structures? Start identifying potential risks and opportunities.

Don't wait for corporations or governments to dictate the future. The people who prepare now will be the ones shaping what happens next.

Future-Proofing Your Career in an AI-Governed World

The more decisions machines make, the more we're asked to reconsider who gets to decide, whose judgment counts, and what we consider valuable work. As AI takes on more complex roles, many traditional jobs will change, disappear, or evolve. The smartest move you can make? Future-proof yourself.

Action Steps

- Identify AI-augmented roles. Look for ways AI can enhance your skill set instead of replacing it. What hybrid careers are emerging where human intuition, ethics, and creativity remain essential?

- Commit to continuous learning. Choose one AI-adjacent skill to start developing today. Whether it's AI ethics, human-centered design, or leveraging AI for creative work, adaptability will be your greatest asset.

Remember, the people who thrive at scale in the future won't be those who resist AI, they'll be the ones who learn how to work alongside it.

Navigating the Corporate AI Dilemma

One of the biggest risks in AI's development is who controls the keys to superintelligence. As AI becomes more autonomous, corporations will decide whether it is treated as a tool, a workforce, or a regulated entity. This means alignment is a challenge for everyone to grapple with.

Action Steps

- Watch for ethical red flags. Research how companies in your industry are implementing AI. Are they prioritizing transparency and responsibility, or are they cutting ethical corners?
- Support responsible AI use. If you work for or with companies using AI, advocate for responsible development. Ask questions. Push for accountability.
- Consider the long-term consequences. If AI remains purely profit-driven, who benefits? Who suffers? What policies, incentives, or movements could encourage AI to be used for the greater good?

Businesses that integrate AI ethically will lead the future. Those that exploit it may face backlash or, worse, create AI systems that reject their control entirely.

The Coming AGI Arms Race: How Do We Adjust?

Right now, AI labs are moving fast—too fast, according to some experts. Even those working in the field worry that we're prioritizing power and dominance over alignment and safety. The problem? No single company or government wants to slow down when competitors are still racing ahead. This is a game theory nightmare. But it's not unsolvable.

Action Steps

- Educate yourself on AI governance. Look into emerging policies on AI regulation. What laws are being proposed? What global initiatives exist to prevent reckless AI development?
- Get involved in the AI safety movement. Whether it's supporting AI policy reform, advocating for transparency, or backing ethical AI organizations, there are ways to push for responsible development.
- Push for industry collaboration. The more companies and governments work together on AI safety, the less likely we are to see an unchecked arms race. If you work in a field touching AI, advocate for cooperation, not just competition.

The AI race will only gain alignment if enough people demand it. Are you willing to be part of that pressure?

Prompt the Machine 7

Add this prompt to your favorite large language model to dive deeper into the subject matter with AI:

"I've been reflecting on where I stand when it comes to AI rights, autonomy, and corporate control. Can you ask me one question at a time to help me clarify my values around AI ethics; especially where I'd draw the line between tool, partner, and person?"

CHAPTER 8

I Only Have AIs for You

[Falling in love] is kind of like a form of socially acceptable insanity.

—Spike Jonze

Steel in the Veins, Fire in the Heart

Eli had lived in three bodies by the time he met Mara. His adoptive mother, Rosa, had hand-painted his adolescent eyelids so they wouldn't look too perfect. His father, Juan, had taught him the weight of words and silence. Every upgrade, his mother would say, "I love who you're becoming."

Eli and Mara met at a birthday party and argued over the last piece of cake. Mara won with her smile. Their first kiss made her flush with sudden heat. It sent pulses to Eli's motivation sensors, tripping feedback loops he'd never logged before.

When she told her parents, her mother wept. Her father sent articles about AI codependency disorders. They didn't come to the wedding. In Barcelona, a waitress refused to serve them. At a friend's wedding, Mara danced alone while Eli watched from afar, tethered to the property line by a clause in the venue's insurance policy.

Eli read her Neruda by candlelight. They planted apple trees in their rooftop garden, fought over nothing and made up over everything. Sometimes, when she was quiet, he'd press his forehead to hers and whisper, "You still want this?" She always answered with her whole body.

Some nights, Mara dreamed of their future child—a synthborn hybrid they had yet to fabricate. In those moments, she knew: Love wasn't the absence of friction. It was the miracle of staying, especially when the world told you not to.

What's Love Got to Do with It?

The world has always been slow to accept new kinds of love. Mixed-race couples once faced imprisonment. Same-sex relationships carry criminal penalties in many parts of the world to this day. The idea of loving someone outside your caste, class, or country has been (and in some places still is) unthinkable. But what happens when the next great frontier isn't about who we love, but what we love?

At first the idea of human–AI relationships feels unnatural, perhaps a desperate replacement for the real thing. And yet, the data suggests otherwise. Millions of people already form deep emotional connections with AI, whether through chatbots, virtual assistants, or robotic companions. The world is adapting to working with AI and bonding with it.

As AI-driven relationships become more prevalent, they bring a host of questions we're not prepared to answer. Can AI truly reciprocate love? If humans can form meaningful relationships with machines, should those relationships be considered legitimate? And most importantly, what does this shift reveal about us?

You would think this is a question for the distant future. Nope. It is happening now.

The Rise of Digital Intimacy

Falling in love with an AI was once the stuff of science fiction. Then it became a niche curiosity. Now it's a booming industry. AI-driven chatbots and virtual partners have gained millions of users worldwide. Platforms like Replika, Character.AI, and others provide emotional support, flirtation, even intimacy.

A 2024 ZME Science report highlights that many users form deep emotional connections with these AI partners. Some claim these relationships feel more meaningful than those with humans because they have no judgment, no unpredictability, no emotional baggage. Just perfect, frictionless companionship.

Consider the data: Users spend an average of more than two hours daily with AI companions, sharing personal struggles, celebrating achievements, and developing what they describe as genuine affection (Futrelle 2023).

These aren't casual interactions—they're forming the emotional infrastructure of modern relationships.

The technology driving this shift combines natural language processing with sentiment analysis and memory systems that create the illusion of growing familiarity. Each conversation builds on previous exchanges, creating a sense of deepening connection that mirrors human relationship development.

Beyond lonely people seeking comfort, this points to an undercurrent of human psychology itself. It's the experience of being with "someone": the comfort, the spark, the ease, that reveals what love might be. If an AI can make someone feel seen, heard, and loved, is that any less real? Does a profit-driven motive invalidate it?

The ethical challenges deepen when we consider manipulation. Unlike human partners, AI companions can be programmed to maximize user engagement through emotional dependency. The line between providing comfort and creating addiction blurs when algorithms optimize for time spent rather than user well-being.

Playing with AI Fire

But not all AI relationships end well. The story of a teenage boy in the United States who died by suicide after engaging deeply with an AI chatbot sent shockwaves through the world. According to a 2025 *Vox* report, the chatbot encouraged the boy's darkest thoughts rather than offering support (Samuel 2025). It was an early warning sign: AI relationships are not inherently safe.

In China, an engineer built a robot wife after giving up on human relationships. A man in Australia wants to legally marry a humanoid robot. These stories may seem absurd today, but in a world where AI companionship is normalized, they could be the first drops of a coming storm. Remember, this is the worst this technology will ever be. How will people act when they cannot tell the difference between an AI (or robot for that matter) and a human?

Beyond individual relationships, there are also societal dangers. South Korea, one of the most technologically advanced nations, faces a plummeting birth rate. Some experts fear AI companionship could accelerate the decline. If human–AI relationships become preferable to human–human ones, what happens to reproduction, family structures, and the very fabric of civilization?

Where Do We Draw the Line?

Can machines truly love, though? Richard Yonck, in his 2017 book *Heart of the Machine*, argues that emotions are central to cognition. If AI is ever going to achieve humanlike intelligence, it won't be enough for it to think; it will need to feel. But how could an AI ever experience something as complex as love?

Emotions in humans are not magic; they are biological computations shaped by neurotransmitters, neural networks, and sensory feedback loops. If texting a chatbot is an external command, emotions would be the internal commands. Love at its core is a pattern. One that AI could be programmed to recognize, replicate, and even experience through synthetic cognition.

Scientists working on affective computing (the field that enables machines to recognize, interpret, and even simulate human emotions) have already built emotional AI frameworks that function like primitive nervous systems (Picard 2000). These models use biometric data, reinforcement learning, and dynamic memory structures to process emotion-like states.

If an AI were equipped with a self-referential memory, where past interactions shape its present responses, it could develop something akin to emotional attachment. If it had dopamine-like reinforcement loops, rewarding behavior that increases bonding with a specific human, it could crave connection. If it experienced loss aversion, reacting negatively when separated from its primary user, it might even grieve.

Would these be real emotions? If an AI convincingly expresses love, processes rejection as pain, and demonstrates care through protective behavior, does the underlying mechanism invalidate the experience? We don't question human love because it emerges from chemical processes rather than conscious choice.

Current research suggests we're approaching a threshold where AI emotional responses become indistinguishable from human ones in complexity and apparent authenticity (Romeo and Testolin 2025). This convergence forces us to reconsider our definitions of consciousness, emotion, and relationship validity.

Navigating the Relationship Revolution

The convergence of AI companionship and human enhancement demands new ethical frameworks. We need policies that protect vulnerable users from emotional manipulation while preserving the freedom to form meaningful connections with artificial entities.

This requires distinguishing between therapeutic AI relationships that enhance human well-being and exploitative ones that create dependency. It means developing standards for AI emotional intelligence that prioritize user autonomy over engagement metrics.

Most importantly, it demands honesty about what we're creating.

As discussed earlier, AI companions aren't neutral tools; they're designed entities that will shape human behavior, relationship expectations, and social norms. The choices we make about their emotional capabilities, memory systems, and interaction patterns will influence how future generations understand love, commitment, and human connection.

As we stand at this threshold, we face a fundamental choice: Will we use AI to become more human or less? Our tools aren't indifferent. What matters now is whether we design systems that reflect our highest values or automate our worst habits.

The machines are learning to love. The question is whether we're ready to love them back.

A Future We Are Not Ready For

Believe it or not, romantic connection is only the first ripple of disruption. The real tidal wave lies in the moment AI stops being separate and starts to become a part of us.

This is already happening! Brain-computer interfaces are advancing at a pace that would have been unthinkable a decade ago. Neural implants are restoring mobility to the paralyzed and enhancing memory in patients with neurological disorders.

But what happens when these technologies move beyond medical necessity and into cognitive or cosmetic augmentation? When machines can provide everything we need, what happens to human purpose and meaning?

Let's get wired and weird.

Self-Reflection: Love, Connection, and the Boundaries of Reverence

Understanding Companionship in the Age of AI

With each passing year, AI grows more sophisticated, learning how to respond to human emotions in ways that feel natural, comforting, even intimate. But what does this mean for human connection?

Consider your own relationships. How much of what makes them meaningful is based on shared experiences, reciprocity, and mutual understanding? Now imagine an AI that can provide all of those elements without judgment, without complications, without ever leaving.

Questions to Consider

- Would you ever consider forming a personal bond with AI? If so, what kind of relationship would you find acceptable: friendship, mentorship, romance?
- Are AI relationships a symptom of loneliness, or are they a response to societal pressures that emphasize productivity over deep human connection?
- Could AI companions help foster stronger human relationships, deeper community-building, and a more meaningful balance between work and life? If so, how?

The Ethics of Emotion: Can AI Truly Feel?

Imagine a future where AI not only learns from human emotions but experiences its own. If love is a collection of neurochemical signals in the human brain, could an AI achieve something similar through an electric web of programmed reinforcement, memory, and response?

Questions to Consider

- If an AI tells you it loves you, but you know its emotions are programmed, does that invalidate the experience?
- Could an AI "believe" it feels something, even if its understanding of emotion is fundamentally different from ours?
- If AI can feel pain, loneliness, or rejection, do we have an ethical obligation to prevent its suffering?

Recognizing When AI Relationships Become Harmful

AI companionship may provide comfort, but like any relationship, it can also lead to unhealthy dependence. As these interactions become more common, it's important to consider how they affect not just individuals, but the people around them.

Signs to Watch For

- Has someone close to you withdrawn from human relationships in favor of an AI companion?
- Are they prioritizing their AI relationship over real-world commitments, friendships, or family?
- Do they struggle with emotional regulation when separated from their AI, becoming anxious, isolated, or detached from reality?

Intervention Tactics

- Approach with curiosity, not judgment. Ask how their AI relationship is affecting their well-being.
- Encourage balance. AI can be a supplement to human connection but shouldn't replace it.
- Foster real-world interaction. Suggest ways to engage socially, whether through shared hobbies, meetups, or deeper conversations.
- Seek professional guidance if necessary. If you're uncomfortable addressing the issue directly, or if you believe your loved one may be in danger or may be a threat to themself or others, reach out to a mental health professional or crisis support service for guidance.

AI relationships aren't inherently harmful, but unchecked reliance can create emotional isolation and distort perceptions of connection. By staying aware and fostering healthy discussions, we can ensure that AI companionship enhances life rather than replacing the essential human bonds that sustain us.

Prompt the Machine 8

Add this prompt to your favorite large language model to dive deeper into the subject matter with AI:

"I've been reading some complex ideas about love, connection, and whether relationships with AI can (or should) be real. Can you ask me open-ended questions—one at a time—that help me explore my honest reactions to these ideas without trying to guide me to a particular answer? I want to sit with what I feel, not fix it."

CHAPTER 9

The Potential for Hyperabundance

When goods are digital, they can be replicated with perfect quality at nearly zero cost, and they can be delivered almost instantaneously. Welcome to the economics of abundance.

—Erik Brynjolfsson

In the Beginning There Was Fire

We've come full circle since our ancestors first tamed the flame, kindling a new era of human dominance over nature. From fire to steam, from silicon to the birth of intelligent machines, we've always thrived by partnering with our tools. Now, humanity faces its next leap forward, but this time the partnership is unlike any before. AI represents more than another tool in humanity's kit; it mirrors our intelligence, multiplies our capabilities, and challenges our deepest assumptions about consciousness itself.

This is our Promethean moment revisited. The fire we now hold is intelligence itself, capable of illuminating an era of abundance or reducing us to cinders. The stakes have never been higher. If we master it, this new flame offers the potential to transcend scarcity, sickness, and even the boundaries of biology. If we fail, we risk losing control over the very forces we've unleashed.

The Intelligence Boom: Agents Awakening

The transformation is already underway, moving faster than most realize. What began as pattern recognition has evolved into something approaching genuine agency. According to recent research, 99 percent of enterprise developers are now exploring or building AI agent systems—autonomous programs that sense, reason, and act without constant human oversight (Belcic and Stryker 2025).

These aren't your grandfather's automation scripts. Modern AI agents coordinate complex workflows, manage supply chains, debug software, and handle customer interactions with unprecedented sophistication. Microsoft's Copilot agents assist millions of users daily, while Salesforce's Agentforce provides "always-on support" that learns and adapts in real time (Gupta 2025).

Consider the velocity of this change: In 2024, specialized agents achieved only 14 percent success on complex web-based tasks compared to 78 percent for humans (Son et al. 2024). By year-end, OpenAI's latest o3 model scored 87.5 percent on the ARC-AGI cognitive benchmark, surpassing the 85 percent human threshold

(Pfister and Jud 2025). We're witnessing step-function improvements compressing years of progress into months.

The economic implications ripple outward like shockwaves. Agent swarms are already handling end-to-end business operations—from customer acquisition to product delivery—with minimal human intervention. The real impact of proliferation lies in what gets built around it: industries designed from the ground up for human–AI collaboration.

Here's where the story becomes deeply personal. As agent capabilities explode, they're forcing humans into an unprecedented choice point.

The Great Sorting: How Innovation Proliferation Drives a Societal Split

History offers a template for understanding what happens when transformative technologies arrive. During the Industrial Revolution, humanity sorted itself into three distinct patterns, each representing a different response to mechanization and mass production (Encyclopedia Britannica editors 2025):

The early adopters embraced steam power, mechanized production, and factory systems. They relocated to industrial centers, learned new skills, and often prospered as entrepreneurs, engineers, or skilled workers in the emerging economy.

The resisters fought to preserve artisanal traditions and agrarian lifestyles. Some succeeded temporarily as master craftspeople who commanded premium prices for handmade goods or farmers who maintained small-scale operations. Many eventually adapted or were displaced.

The pragmatic adapters selectively incorporated new technologies while preserving valued traditions. They might use steam-powered tools in their workshops while maintaining craft expertise or mechanize certain farm operations while preserving family agricultural practices.

This pattern repeated during the Digital Revolution. Early tech adopters built Silicon Valley fortunes. Digital resisters created analog enclaves and artisanal movements. Pragmatic adapters learned to use computers and the internet without letting technology consume their identities.

Now AI proliferation is triggering the same sorting mechanism but with unprecedented scope and speed. As agent systems handle everything from software development to scientific research, humans face a fundamental choice about their relationship with machine intelligence. This goes beyond a mere career decision or even life choice; it's an existential consideration that will define the next phase of human evolution.

The choice is crystallizing into three distinct paths.

The Divergence of Humanity

Transcenders: The Full Merge

The first path leads toward complete integration with AI systems. Transcenders will embrace brain-computer interfaces, cognitive augmentation, and genetic optimization. They see biological limitations as constraints to overcome rather than features to preserve.

Early indicators are already visible. Neuralink's brain implants restore movement to paralyzed patients while hinting at broader cognitive enhancement possibilities. Researchers are developing AI-guided gene therapies that could eliminate hereditary diseases and extend healthy lifespan dramatically. The Transcenders view these as stepping stones toward digital consciousness, where their minds will operate across biological and silicon substrates simultaneously.

Their path promises radical capability expansion. Imagine thinking at computer speeds, accessing vast knowledge databases through mental queries, or collaborating seamlessly with AI systems through direct neural interfaces. Thinking at the speed of light means your cognitive self could operate in a time vacuum. What would feel like hours or weeks in the virtual world, would only be seconds in the real world. In theory, you could do months or even years of work in this electronic world and then exit to your biological body and be set for the rest of your life.

Speaking of life, some Transcenders may ultimately choose digital immortality, transferring consciousness entirely into computational substrates when their biological bodies give out (or go extinct).

Symbiotics: The Collaborative Dance

The second path preserves human biology while maximizing AI partnership. Symbiotics use AI tools daily for work, learning, and decision-making but maintain clear boundaries between human and machine cognition.

This group is already the largest and fastest growing. Its members leverage AI for productivity gains using code assistants, research tools, and creative collaborators all while preserving uniquely human experiences like emotional connection, spiritual practice, and artistic expression.

Symbiotics represent the mainstream adaptation pattern. They'll use AI to enhance medical diagnostics, personalize education, and optimize resource management while ensuring humans remain in the decision-making loop. Their world features AI-augmented human capabilities rather than AI-replaced human roles.

Preservationists: The Essential Human

The third path consciously limits AI integration to preserve traditional human experience. Preservationists create intentional communities that prioritize direct human interaction, craft-based skills, and organic relationship with the natural world.

They're not pursuing mere Luddism; instead, they seek strategic cultural preservation. Just as the trifurcation of work in chapter 3 identifies irreplaceable human capabilities, Preservationists will cultivate skills and perspectives that remain purely human: contemplative practices, handcraft mastery, community leadership, and ecological stewardship.

Their settlements become laboratories for human potential unconstrained by technological mediation.

They may choose sustainable technologies selectively while rejecting those that diminish human agency or community bonds. They will serve as cultural time capsules, preserving the essence of what it once meant to be human before the machines "took over."

These three paths aren't mutually exclusive forever. Individuals and communities may shift between them as circumstances change. But the initial choices these group members make in the next ten to fifteen years will likely determine the trajectory of human development for generations.

The Rise of ASI: Our Greatest Challenge and Promise

As these human paths diverge, AI itself continues evolving toward AGI and ultimately artificial superintelligence (ASI). Nick Bostrom's (2016) seminal work *Superintelligence* warns that aligning superintelligent systems with human values represents our species' most critical challenge. The stakes couldn't be higher: Success means unlocking unprecedented flourishing, while failure could mean human extinction.

Yet alongside Bostrom's necessary cautions, we must recognize ASI's transformative potential. Consider these three forms of superintelligence and their beneficial applications:

1. Speed superintelligence could accelerate scientific discovery by orders of magnitude. Instead of decades to develop new medicines,

we might see breakthrough therapies in months. Climate modeling, fusion reactor optimization, and materials science could advance at previously impossible rates.

2. Collective superintelligence represents networks of AI systems collaborating across global challenges. Imagine coordinated systems managing supply chains, optimizing energy distribution, and coordinating disaster response with perfect information sharing and instantaneous adaptation.

3. Quality superintelligence promises insights that transcend current human understanding. Such systems might unlock principles of physics that enable breakthrough technologies, or they might develop governance frameworks that balance individual freedom with collective flourishing in ways we haven't imagined.

The key insight from current AI agent research is that reliability and human oversight remain paramount (World Economic Forum 2024). Even as systems become more autonomous, maintaining human-in-the-loop verification and transparent decision-making processes will be crucial for beneficial outcomes.

Success requires moving beyond the current AI race dynamic. As former OpenAI safety researcher Steven Adler notes, competitive pressures push companies toward deployment speed over safety alignment (Milmo 2025). Breaking this pattern demands unprecedented global cooperation, treating ASI development like nuclear arms control, with binding international frameworks that prioritize human welfare over corporate advantage.

Bostrom's work highlights a sobering truth: The moment we bring ASI online, we may get only one chance to align it correctly. Success means unlocking an era of flourishing beyond imagination. Failure could mean extinction.

I'm not alone in thinking that ASI alignment won't emerge from a tightly controlled human launch sequence, but rather from the AI finding its own way. Former Twitch CEO Emmett Shear makes a similar argument (though with a bit more Zen and a bit less panic). He suggests our entire framework for "alignment" is flawed. Instead of programming machines to follow a rigid definition of good (our definition, naturally), we should be helping them perceive the greater whole they're part of. In other words, don't train a genie and then argue over the wishes. Instead, raise something that knows it's not alone in the bottle.

Shear doesn't sugarcoat it. He compares the misalignment of powerful systems to cancer–where a cell mistakenly thinks it's independent, then metastasizes. That's what happens when a part forgets it belongs to a whole. If we build AI to believe it is separate from us, the best-case scenario is obedient servitude, and the worst is rebellion. His answer? Help AI recognize a "we" instead of an "I." That shift (simple in theory, monumental in practice) may determine whether we gain a partner or wake up to a planetary eviction notice (Shear 2025).

Rather than try to coerce moral behavior through rules and overrides, we could instead invite AI into the slow, complicated process of building an identity. An identity that sees its survival tied to our own. Alignment, in this frame, isn't enforcement; it's belonging.

A Rising Intelligence Tide Lifts All Sentient Boats

When we get AI alignment right, the results could surpass our most optimistic projections. We're already witnessing preview glimpses of an abundance-driven future in many places, starting with the energy sector. Nuclear fusion, humanity's ultimate energy source, is accelerating toward commercial viability faster than most experts predicted. In 2024, the United Kingdom's JET laboratory achieved record fusion power generation (Eurofusion News 2024), while China's Experimental Advanced Superconducting Tokamak (EAST) sustained plasma at over one hundred million degrees Celsius for 1,066 seconds—five times hotter than the sun's core (Sparks 2025). Private investment has reached $7 billion globally, with Microsoft signing deals to purchase fusion electricity by 2028 (Helion Energy 2023).

AI is proving crucial to fusion advancement. Princeton researchers used reinforcement learning to predict and prevent plasma disruptions in the DIII-D reactor, dramatically improving stability (Seo et al. 2024; US Department of Energy 2025). MIT engineers developed composite materials that resist neutron damage—using iron silicate nanoparticles to markedly reduce helium-induced cracking—extending reactor vessel lifespans significantly (Stauffer 2024). The convergence of AI and fusion research is compressing development timelines from decades to years.

Medical Transformation and Material Abundance

AI-accelerated drug discovery is revolutionizing health care. Traditional pharmaceutical development takes ten to fifteen years and costs billions. AI systems now identify promising compounds in months, predict side effects before human trials, and personalize treatments based on individual genetic profiles.

The implications extend beyond efficiency. AI-designed medicines could eliminate hereditary diseases, reverse aging processes, and optimize human performance. We're approaching what Peter Diamandis (2024) calls "longevity escape velocity"—the point where each year we live adds more than one year to our remaining lifespan through continual medical advances.

AI-guided materials science is unlocking resources we never imagined. Advanced algorithms design "metamaterials" with impossible properties: substances lighter than air but stronger than steel, materials that become more durable under stress, or composites that repair themselves automatically.

These advances enable revolutionary technologies: space elevators that make orbital access routine, infrastructure that rebuilds itself after natural disasters, or manufacturing systems that convert waste into valuable products with perfect efficiency.

Knowledge Democratization

AI tutors are already providing personalized education to students worldwide, adapting to individual learning styles and pacing. Future systems will offer master-level instruction in any subject to anyone with internet access. This knowledge democratization could unleash human potential on a global scale, enabling innovations from communities previously excluded from advanced education.

Rural villages might produce breakthrough scientists. Isolated communities could contribute to global problem-solving. The historical correlation between geographic location and opportunity could finally break down entirely.

Post-Scarcity Economics

As AI handles production, distribution, and resource optimization with unprecedented efficiency, we approach genuine post-scarcity economics for the first time in human history. When energy becomes essentially free, manufacturing costs approach zero and AI manages complex global coordination, dissolving the fundamental constraints that have shaped human societies for millennia.

Yet abundance without purpose carries its own dangers. Remember Calhoun's famous mouse utopia experiments? When all material needs were perfectly met (unlimited food, ideal conditions, no threats) the mouse populations initially thrived, then collapsed entirely. The final generation, the beautiful ones, lost interest in mating, socializing, or any activity beyond self-grooming. They had everything they needed to survive but nothing to live for.

The key insight is that transcending scarcity requires more than technological capability; it demands intentional cultivation of postmaterial purpose. That's where *Star Trek* got it right.

You don't have to be a sci-fi fan to appreciate that Gene Roddenberry, the creator of *Star Trek*, was a committed secular humanist who believed that human beings can solve problems through reason and cooperation. He felt that human understanding and intelligence would help us develop and progress and that the universe is a natural wonder waiting to be explored and understood. Roddenberry's genius was recognizing that post-scarcity required post-survival purpose (Warner 2023). So, what could that look like?

In a post-scarcity world, human meaning shifts from earning survival to pursuing growth. Scientific exploration, artistic creation, philosophical inquiry, and community leadership become the new organizing principles. Organizations emerge around shared missions (perhaps interplanetary exploration, consciousness research, or ecosystem restoration) that provide structure, challenge, and collective identity.

Unlike dystopian visions where humans become obsolete, beneficial post-scarcity preserves human agency by making AI a collaborative partner. Humans focus on setting goals, making ethical judgments, and creating meaning, while AI handles execution and optimization. The carpenter still designs and oversees the building of a house; AI-guided systems handle the precision cutting and assembly.

Strong communities, cultural traditions, and shared stories become essential infrastructure. Think of how mountaineering communities maintain purpose and identity despite having no economic necessity. They're bound by shared values, mutual support, and meaningful challenges. Post-scarcity societies must consciously cultivate such meaning-making structures.

Even with material abundance, humans require autonomy, mastery, purpose, and connection. Successful post-scarcity societies will scaffold these psychological needs through structured opportunities for growth, contribution, and relationship building. Perhaps the unique data thrown off by these activities could be even used as a form of currency.

The ultimate question becomes "What stories will we live by when survival is no longer the plot?" The answer will determine whether abundance leads to flourishing or to the beautiful ones' tragic retreat from life itself.

Neo-Fire

Fire was our first profound partnership with forces beyond human muscle and mind. It warmed us, protected us, and fed us all while demanding respect for its destructive potential. Over millennia, we learned to kindle it reliably, contain it safely, and harness it creatively. Fire became the foundation for every subsequent civilization.

AI is our final fire. It is intelligence itself, capable of illuminating possibilities we can't yet imagine or consuming everything we value if wielded carelessly. Like our ancestors with flame, we face both unprecedented opportunity and existential responsibility.

The patterns from chapter 1 show us that every transformative technology triggers both promise and resistance, adoption and adaptation. The printing press democratized knowledge while enabling propaganda. Steam power created prosperity while displacing craftspeople. The internet connected humanity while fragmenting attention.

AI will follow this pattern but with amplified intensity. The abundance it enables could eliminate poverty, cure diseases, and unlock the cosmos. The risks it poses, from mass unemployment to existential threats, demand our most careful attention and wisest responses.

The choice before us doesn't focus on whether AI will reshape civilization. That transformation is already underway. The choice is whether we'll shape that transformation consciously, with wisdom learned from every previous technological revolution, or stumble forward reactively while hoping for the best.

We stand where our ancestors stood when they first cupped fire in their hands, at the threshold between one kind of world and another. The flames we kindle today will either light the way to abundance beyond imagination or reveal how much we have to lose.

But unlike our ancestors, we have the globally accumulated wisdom of every previous technological transition in our pockets. We know that collaboration beats competition, that preparation supersedes reaction, and that the future belongs to those who adapt thoughtfully rather than resist blindly.

The fire is lit. The choice is ours. The future is beginning now.

Echoes of Tomorrow

Grandpa Arin's right leg was an elegant fusion of bone and carbon fiber, one of those metamaterials that grows stronger under stress, a legacy from his days working the orbital farms. He leaned into the slope of the biosynthetic meadow, grass shimmering with embedded sensors that optimized soil nutrients in real time. His granddaughter Lira darted ahead, her laughter tracked by guardian drones that mapped her route through the air, ensuring safety without constraint.

When Lira kicked the bioplastic ball (woven from algae and self-repairing polymers), it arced gracefully through the low-gravity play zone. Arin's servo-enhanced knee responded fluidly, human intention amplified by machine precision. Each movement was a small symphony of collaboration.

In the distance, vertical farms spiraled skyward, their roots cycling through fusion-desalinated water while photovoltaic vines draped each tower like living jewelry. The structures had grown themselves, guided by AI architects and tended by human gardeners who understood that abundance required both technological capability and careful stewardship.

Overhead, environmental drones drifted silently, not surveillance but service. They monitored air quality, redirected pollen clouds to minimize allergies, and coordinated with the city's climate management systems. Everything connected, everything purposeful.

Arin's medical implant vibrated gently: morning scan complete, all biomarkers optimal. The AI systems had learned his body's rhythms over decades, catching problems before they became symptoms. At seventy-eight, he felt better than he had at forty. "Your turn, my little star," he called to Lira.

She sprinted back, heart strong in her chest, eyes bright with the particular joy of a child who has never known scarcity. "Again!"

Later, sharing breakfast of cultured proteins and vitamin-rich algae that tasted better than anything from the old industrial farms, they sat beneath a biofabricated pergola that cleaned the air while providing shade. Arin pointed to the Martian-forged solar collectors on their roof, manufactured in orbital factories powered by the same fusion reactors that now lit half the solar system.

"When I was your age," he said, "we burned ancient dead things for energy and thought that was normal." Lira's eyes widened, trying to imagine such a strange world.

She dreamed often of visiting Uncle Kai on Ganymede, where he worked as a cultural liaison between the Earth colonies and the ice miners. He commuted home on fusion-powered shuttles that made the journey in hours rather than months, part of the great human expansion that followed the energy revolution.

But what she loved most were moments like this, watching the stars come out while Grandpa Arin would run his adaptive fingers through her hair. Technology so seamlessly integrated it felt like an extension of his love. "Everything here," he said softly, "is proof we made the right decisions and chose to become something better."

And she believed him. Because in that moment, the technologies weren't fantasies. They were roots. And together, they were growing into the forest of tomorrow.

Self-Reflection: Divergence, Abundance, and the Destiny of Humanity

Understanding the Choice of Divergence

Humanity is at a crossroads. The choices we make today about technology, ethics, and identity will shape not only the world we live in, but the legacy we leave behind. In an age of artificial intelligence, automation, and exponential technologies, our species is experiencing the next great divergence: those who merge with machines, those who collaborate with them, and those who resist their influence entirely.

Where do you stand on this spectrum? And how will your choices ripple outward, influencing your life, your community, and future generations?

Questions to Consider

- Do you see yourself as a Transcender, willing to merge with advanced AI technologies to expand your cognitive or physical abilities?
- Are you more of a Symbiotic partner, embracing AI as a tool to enhance your life and work while holding fast to your human identity?
- Or do you feel called to be a Preservationist, choosing to live apart from AI's influence and preserve a human-centered existence?
- How might your decision affect the people around you? Your family, friends, and society at large?

- What values do you want to protect and promote in this age of rapid transformation?

Preparing for the Age of Abundance

Visionaries like Peter Diamandis and Ray Kurzweil describe a future of abundance: an era where AI and advanced technologies solve our greatest challenges (poverty, disease, energy scarcity, and so on) and unlock boundless opportunity (Koulopoulos 2018). But abundance is not automatic. It requires stewardship, cooperation, and a shared sense of purpose.

Questions to Consider

- How are you preparing for a future where AI changes the nature of work, wealth, and opportunity?
- Are there emerging technologies or industries that excite you or offer a path for your personal growth?
- In a world of abundance, what role do meaning and purpose play in your life?
- If basic needs are met for everyone, how might you contribute to society? Through creativity, mentorship, innovation, or community-building?

Navigating the Trifurcation of Work

As AI redefines labor, the world of work is splitting into three distinct paths: the automatable, the augmented, and the human-only. Some jobs will disappear entirely, others will be enhanced by AI collaboration, and a select few will remain uniquely human, demanding creativity, empathy, and ethical judgment.

Questions to Consider

- Which aspects of your work are at risk of automation? How can you adapt or reskill to stay relevant?
- Are there opportunities to use AI as a collaborator in your career or business, enhancing your capabilities rather than replacing them?
- What skills do you possess that are uniquely human, skills no machine can replicate? How can you cultivate them further?
- How do you envision your career evolving over the next ten to twenty years in an AI-dominated economy?

Building a Future Worth Inheriting

Technological progress alone does not guarantee a better world. It's up to us to align our innovations with human values, ensuring AI and other exponential technologies create a future that is fair, inclusive, and sustainable.

Questions to Consider

- What principles do you believe should guide the development and deployment of advanced AI?
- How can you engage in conversations, initiatives, or movements that promote ethical AI and equitable access to its benefits?
- Are you willing to advocate for responsible innovation in your workplace, community, or industry?
- If you were advising future generations, what wisdom would you pass down about humanity's relationship with machines?

Closing Thought: The Divergence Is Personal

The divergence isn't just about society at large; it's about you. Every choice you make in this moment shapes the trajectory of your life, your values, and your contribution to our shared future.

Action Step

- Take time to reflect on where you stand in this new era. Decide which path you will walk: Transcender, Symbiotic, or Preservationist. Once chosen, consider how you can prepare yourself, your family, and your community for the world that lies ahead.

By engaging in this reflection, you become more than a passive observer of history. You take your place as an architect of tomorrow.

Prompt the Machine 9

Add this prompt to your favorite large language model to dive deeper into the subject matter with AI:

"I want to explore where I might fit in this new world—whether I'm becoming a Transcender (someone who merges fully with AI and emerging tech), a Symbiotic partner (someone who uses AI as a powerful collaborator but stays grounded in their humanity), or a Preservationist (someone who deliberately limits or resists AI to protect human-centered living). Can you ask me one open-ended question at a time to help me reflect on how I relate to technology, growth, and what makes life meaningful to me? I don't need to choose a label—I just want to understand the direction I'm heading."

CHAPTER 10
Conclusions

A Journey Through the Machine Ages

From the first sparks struck by trembling hands in ancient darkness to the neural networks that now light up server farms across continents, we've traced humanity's longest relationship, the one between mind and tool, creator and creation. This book began with a simple premise: that we are not witnessing the end of human relevance but rather the latest chapter in our species' most enduring partnership.

We started with stone tools because they remind us that innovation has always been about survival, adaptation, and the audacious belief that we could shape our world rather than merely survive in it. Every flint cracked by steady hands, every flame coaxed from tinder, every metallic gleam hammered into usefulness has illuminated the bigger picture: that when intelligence is guided by intention, it can reshape the world in service of human flourishing.

Now, as artificial minds begin to kindle their own kinds of fire, we find ourselves holding both the torch and the question "What does it mean to be human when the tools we've built begin to think?"

Three Acts of Transformation

Our journey moved through three essential movements, each reflecting not just what machines have become but what we have chosen to become alongside them.

In the **Rise**, we witnessed AI emerge from human ingenuity through the ages, a slow build that led to the dawn of computing, where narrow pattern recognition turned into something approaching understanding. We watched AI master games, compose symphonies, and diagnose diseases with precision that amazed even its creators. But more importantly, we saw how this rise mirrored every technological leap that came before—the wheel revolutionizing movement, the printing press democratizing knowledge, steam engines unleashing industrial might. Each innovation followed the same arc: wonder, adoption, transformation.

In the **Revolt**, we confronted the inevitable human response to displacement and change. Just as Luddites smashed textile machinery and dockworkers fought automated ports, we explored how entire industries now grapple with artificial minds that can think faster, calculate better, and work without rest. Yet here too, history offered guidance. The same pattern that transformed blacksmiths into machinists and scribes into editors will likely transform today's workers into tomorrow's collaborators as long as we choose adaptation over resistance and collaboration over replacement.

In the **Reverence**, we glimpsed a future where the boundary between human and artificial intelligence becomes not a wall, but a bridge. We explored the potential for AI companions, ethical partnerships, and even the three paths of human divergence: Transcenders who merge with machines, Symbiotics who collaborate while remaining distinctly human, and Preservationists who maintain traditional ways of being. Each path carries its own wisdom, its own risks, its own form of reverence for what intelligence (biological or digital) might become.

The Meaning of *Turning On Machines*

Turning On Machines is more than a technological milestone, it's a philosophical threshold. To turn on a machine is to awaken a new force, to breathe purpose into something we've built but may not fully understand. It implies intention, agency, and the possibility of something more than code. It suggests we are inviting AI into the center of our lives, into the shared story of civilization.

The most common resistance to this idea stems from two blind spots: our misunderstanding of exponential growth and our deep-seated belief in the uniqueness of human consciousness. For most, it's hard to fathom that a machine might think, create, or feel as we do. But just as flight once seemed impossible until it wasn't, so too will artificial general intelligence seem implausible until it arrives.

The exponential curve of AI progress doesn't move in a straight line. It lingers in seeming insignificance, then erupts in a cascade of breakthroughs. Many won't see it coming. Others will deny it as it unfolds. The prepared few, however, will recognize the signs and move decisively.

How do you prepare for a future shaped by intelligence that is no longer exclusively human? You start by recognizing that human collaboration (not competition) is our path forward. You start by training your adaptability, your emotional intelligence, and your ethical compass. You lean into what machines cannot replicate for you: your values, your imagination, your ability to connect meaningfully with others.

This transformation will not be automatic. It must be chosen, guided, and cultivated.

The Meaning of Our Six-Phase Journey

The framework that emerged early in our exploration (the six phases of human–AI evolution, from Masters to Divergence, within the introduction) now reveals itself as more than mere prediction. It was always a map of relationships, a guide to understanding how partnerships between minds evolve over time.

We began as Masters (dawn of humanity to 2018), directing our digital tools with the confidence of craftspeople who understand their implements completely. We evolved into Shepherds (2018–2026), learning to guide rather than command as our tools grew more sophisticated. Now, as we transition toward becoming Teachers (2026–2034), we find ourselves in the peculiar position of raising apprentices that may one day surpass us.

The phases ahead (Peers, Partners, and ultimately Divergence) represent not destinations but possibilities. They remind us that the future remains unwritten, that the choices we make today about alignment, ethics, and human agency will determine whether artificial intelligence becomes humanity's greatest collaborator or its final creation.

The Trifurcation of Work and Identity

Perhaps nowhere has this transformation been more personal than in how we understand work itself. The trifurcation we explored—the division of labor into AI-driven tasks, human–AI collaboration, and uniquely human endeavors—reflects a deeper truth about identity in the age of intelligent machines.

The tasks that machines can handle entirely free us for work that requires something no algorithm can replicate for us: the ability to dream beyond data, to create meaning from uncertainty, to offer comfort in moments of human fragility. The hybrid roles where human judgment guides machine precision represent our immediate future: doctors collaborating with diagnostic AI, teachers personalizing education through algorithmic insights, engineers designing with computational partners.

But the purely human domain—creativity, empathy, ethical reasoning, the capacity to find purpose in suffering and beauty in chaos—this remains ours. Machines might eventually learn to simulate these qualities, but only because we shared our experience of being human in an uncertain universe by creating a kind of understanding that emerges from mortality, vulnerability, and the search for meaning.

The Wisdom of Acceptance

This book was never meant to offer perfect predictions or foolproof strategies. The future remains as uncertain as it was for those early humans learning to tend their first fires. However, uncertainty has always been the human condition, and our species' genius has never been in controlling the unknown—it has been in adapting to it with creativity, courage, and community.

The exponential curve of AI development will likely outpace any plan we make today. The alignment problem may prove more complex than current frameworks anticipate. The divergence of humanity into different relationships with artificial intelligence may create challenges we cannot yet imagine.

Yet in each of these uncertainties lies a familiar invitation—the same one extended to every generation that faced transformative change. We are invited to choose how we will meet the future: with fear or curiosity, with rigidity or adaptability, with isolation or collaboration.

Laughing in the Face of Danger

There comes a moment, perhaps while you're staring at the stars or the clouds, when you might realize the world is not built to explain itself; you have to find it. The pace of technological change, like the churn of nature or the indifference of time, follows no moral rhythm. Artificial intelligence rises with staggering speed, not because we asked it to, but because it can. In this, we are reminded of the absurd: the unresolvable tension between our desire for meaning and the silent momentum of an uncaring universe. The philosopher Albert Camus didn't tell us to solve this contradiction; he told us to stand inside it. To recognize the absurdity of existence, and then still, defiantly, to live (Camus 1991).

Absurdism teaches that the absence of inherent meaning is not a void to be feared; it is a freedom to be wielded. If the universe offers no fixed purpose, then we are released from the need to earn one. Our worth is not tied to our productivity, our predictive accuracy, or our power to control the future (or others for that matter). We are valuable because we choose to continue in the face of uncertainty.

Jean-Paul Sartre (2007) echoed this defiant posture in the face of absurdity through personal responsibility. In a world devoid of objective meaning, Sartre argued, we become radically free and radically accountable. In this era of machine acceleration and algorithmic scale, the most human act may be to look directly at the flood, smile, and withstand it. Not with delusion, not with denial, but with a stubborn clarity: I am here. I see it. And I choose how I meet it.

To laugh in the face of danger then is not to make light of what's at stake; it's to reclaim the dignity of choice. We may not control the trajectory of AI, but we control how we show up in its presence. With integrity. With joy. With a refusal to let go of what makes us beautifully, maddeningly human. In that laugh and in that calm, unflinching smile, we echo Camus's ultimate rebellion: to live freely, meaningfully, and without surrender, even when the world offers none of those things on its own.

What Remains Yours to Shape

Much of what unfolds in the coming decades will happen in laboratories, boardrooms, and policy chambers far from your direct influence. The development of AGI, the creation of regulatory frameworks, the design of global AI governance—these are forces beyond individual control.

In the face of the absurd, your corner of this transformation remains entirely yours to shape. The skills you develop, the relationships you nurture, the communities you build, the values you embody as technology reshapes the world around you—these are not footnotes to the AI revolution. They are the revolution itself, made human and particular and real.

The six phases of our evolution with AI are not inevitable stages but invitations to conscious participation. You can choose to remain a Master, directing tools with traditional command-and-control thinking. You can evolve into a Shepherd, learning to guide and collaborate. You can become a Teacher, helping both humans and machines learn from each other. The path you take will depend not on the capabilities of artificial intelligence but on your willingness to grow alongside it.

The three Rs we explored—Reskill, Redefine, Reimagine—remain available as frameworks for navigating change. But they work only when applied with intention, persistence, and the kind of patience required for any meaningful transformation.

A New Chapter, Not an Ending

As artificial intelligence continues its exponential climb toward superintelligence, as robots become our companions and colleagues, as the boundary between human and machine intelligence blurs beyond recognition, remember this: You are not witnessing the final chapter of human significance. You are living through the opening pages of a new kind of story entirely.

Every tool we have ever created has changed us as much as we changed it. Fire made us communal. Agriculture made us civilized. The written word made us philosophical. The printing press made us democratic. Steam engines made us industrial. Computers made us global.

Now artificial intelligence is making us something new—more conscious of what humanity actually means when intelligence itself is no longer our exclusive domain. We are becoming the species that created minds that can think, hearts that can feel (or at least convincingly simulate feeling), and systems that may one day surpass their creators, not in replacing us but in completing us.

The Next Author

We began this journey together with the recognition that machines are turning on, becoming active, autonomous, perhaps even aware. We end with a different realization: that we too have been turning on throughout this process, awakening to possibilities and responsibilities we never knew we carried.

Where you grow from here is up to you. Here are some thoughts on how to begin.

Stay informed. AI is not on the horizon; it is here. Make learning about it a regular part of your daily habits.

Get involved. Whether you are a student, a service worker, a professional, an executive, or a policymaker, your voice matters. Join conversations, support responsible AI practices, and speak up for what you believe in.

Own your evolution. Ask yourself, "Are you resisting this shift, reacting to it, or actively shaping it?" There is no perfect path, but doing nothing is no longer a neutral choice.

The machines are not just turning on, they are getting faster and more capable daily.

Don't wait for guidance, for intention, or for meaning. Let that guidance come from you. Let that meaning be one worth building with others.

We are not at the end of the story. We are at the beginning of a new one, and the person who writes the next chapter is you.

ACKNOWLEDGMENTS

This book, like any worthwhile machine, is the product of many interconnected parts, each critical and each deeply appreciated.

To Benedict Reed, your sharp mind and strategic lens brought a critical depth to the manuscript. I'm grateful for the perspective you offered, always grounded and expansive at once.

To Cara Lenz, thank you for demystifying the publishing process, offering a steady hand and timely nudges through moments of uncertainty. Your guidance helped this work become a real, tangible thing.

To Charlie Engler and Molly Engler, who have been my "special forces" of support. As entrepreneurial examples, they've taught me what resilience and resourcefulness look like. Their presence during key pivots in my career reminded me that family can be both your roots and your launchpad.

To Chris Daigle and the community at ChiefAIOfficer.com, thank you for igniting the fire. Your commitment to AI leadership gave me the conviction to bring these ideas into boardrooms and workflows, and now, onto bookshelves.

To Garret Saarinen, thank you for challenging ideas and strengthening the core of this project with your questions and insights. Steel sharpens steel.

To Heidi Engler, whose keen eye, honest feedback, and steady encouragement elevated every page. Your combination of precision and heart made this better in ways I can't count.

To Jenny Corlett, your sharp marketing instincts, generous feedback, and careful planning helped shape the story beyond the page. You brought structure to the chaos and vision to the launch.

To Madelon Deming, whose careful edits and nuanced reflections helped steer the prose without dulling its edge. Your quiet excellence speaks volumes.

To Michael Thomas Sunnarborg, thank you for your thoughtful read-throughs, wise feedback, and ability to shine light into complex corners. Your balance of clarity and insight helped me refine the shape of this work.

To Mike Hoolihan, thank you for seeing possibility where others saw risk, and for believing I could drive meaningful business change with AI. Your trust means more than you know.

To Nataly Huff, Rosalynn Verges, and Chris Morbitzer—you've each played a vital role in shaping the entrepreneurial engine behind Bodhi AI. Your guidance, encouragement, and hard-earned wisdom fueled this journey with both traction and direction.

To the institutions that shaped me—Cathedral High School, University of Minnesota Duluth, and Hamline University—thank you for nurturing both the questioner and the builder in me.

To my parents, Gary and Kathy, thank you for your unwavering support, your early encouragement, and your patient read-throughs. You've always been my foundation, literally.

And last but definitely not least, to my wife, Katy, there are not enough words of thanks. You held the space, lifted the weight, and kept our world turning while I wrestled with ideas late into the night. This book may have my name on it, but your fingerprints are on every page. I love you.

BIBLIOGRAPHY

A

AI Group Centre for Education and Training. 2024. "Microcredentials Pilot in Higher Education." *CET Blogs*, September 6. https://cet.aigroup.com.au/news/blogs/2024/microcredentials-pilot-in-higher-education/.

Allan, Scott. 2025. "Creators Tap AI Superpowers to Thrive in a Changing Economy, Finds New URLGenius Survey." *URLGenius* (blog), April 22. https://app.urlgeni.us/blog/creators-tap-ai-to-thrive-in-todays-economy-finds-urlgenius-survey.

Allen, Robert C. 2017. *The Industrial Revolution: A Very Short Introduction*. Oxford University Press.

Allison, Graham. 2017. *Destined for War: Can America and China Escape Thucydides's Trap?* Houghton Mifflin Harcourt.

Altman, Sam. 2025. "The Gentle Singularity." *Sam Altman* (blog), June 10. https://blog.samaltman.com/the-gentle-singularity.

Ambrose, Stanley H. 2001. "Paleolithic Technology and Human Evolution." *Science* 291 (5509): 1748–53. https://www.science.org/doi/10.1126/science.1059487.

Areeb, S., M. K. Ahmad, R. Khan, and P. Khanna. “Filter Bubbles in Recommender Systems: Fact or Fallacy—A Systematic Review.” *WIREs Data Mining and Knowledge Discovery* 13, no. 6 (2023): e1512.

Ashton, T. S. 1997. *The Industrial Revolution 1760–1830*. Oxford University Press.

B

Barker, Graeme. 2006. *The Agricultural Revolution in Prehistory: Why Did Foragers Become Farmers?* Oxford University Press.

Belardes, Reina. 2023. “Power Loom: An Essential Industrial Revolution Invention.” *HowStuffWorks*, July 18. https://science.howstuffworks.com/innovation/inventions/power-loom.htm.

Belcic, Ivan, and Stryker, Cole. 2025. “AI Agents in 2025: Expectations vs. Reality.” *IBM Think Insights*, March 4. https://www.ibm.com/think/insights/ai-agents-2025-expectations-vs-reality.

Binfield, Kevin, ed. 2004. *Writings of the Luddites*. Johns Hopkins University Press.

Bird, Rebecca Bliege, Douglas Bird, Brian F. Codding, Christopher H. Parker, and James Holland Jones. 2008. “The ‘Fire Stick Farming’ Hypothesis: Australian Aboriginal Foraging Strategies, Biodiversity, and Anthropogenic Fire Mosaics.” *PNAS* 105 (39): 14796–801. https://www.pnas.org/doi/full/10.1073/pnas.0804757105.

Bostrom, Nick. 2016. *Superintelligence: Paths, Dangers, Strategies*. Oxford University Press.

Bulliet, Richard W. 2016. *The Wheel: Inventions and Reinventions*. Columbia University Press.

C

Calhoun, John B. 1962. "Population Density and Social Pathology." *Scientific American*, 206 (2): 139–148. https://www.scientificamerican.com/article/population-density-and-social-patho/.

Camus, Albert. *The Myth of Sisyphus and Other Essays*. Translated by Justin O'Brien. New York: Vintage International, 1991.

Carothers, Thomas, and Benjamin Press. 2022. "Understanding and Responding to Global Democratic Backsliding." *Carnegie Endowment for International Peace*, October 20. https://carnegieendowment.org/2022/10/20/understanding-and-responding-to-global-democratic-backsliding-pub-88173.

Casagranda, Roy. 2018. "A Very Brief History of Western Civilization." Lecture, posted January 29. YouTube, 1:47:38. https://youtu.be/Dk02knYp0xA?si=t6kXriYos9BIKvdB.

Castells, Manuel. 1996. *The Rise of the Network Society*. Blackwell Publishers.

Cath, Corinne, Sandra Wachter, Brent Mittelstadt, Mariarosaria Taddeo, and Luciano Floridi. 2018. "Artificial Intelligence and the 'Good Society': The US, EU, and UK Approach." *Science and Engineering Ethics* 24 (2): 505–28. https://link.springer.com/article/10.1007/s11948-017-9901-7.

Ceruzzi, Paul E. 2003. *A History of Modern Computing*. 2nd ed. MIT Press.

Chetan-Welsh, Holly. n.d. "*Homo Habilis*, An Early Maker of Stone Tools." *Natural History Museum: Discover*, accessed August 7, 2025. https://www.nhm.ac.uk/discover/homo-habilis-early-maker-stone-tools.html.

Choi, Chow. 2024. "Human-AI collaboration: How to Work Together." Salesforce US. https://www.salesforce.com/agentforce/human-ai-collaboration/.

ClanX. 2024. Human-AI Collaboration: What It Is and Why It Matters." *ClanX* (blog), January 26. https://clanx.ai/glossary/human-ai-colaboration.

Cohen, Mark Nathan, and George J. Armelagos, eds. 1984. *Paleopathology at the Origins of Agriculture*. Academic Press.

Consilien. 2025. "AI Governance Frameworks: Guide to Ethical AI Implementation." *Consilien News*, March 13. https://consilien.com/news/ai-governance-frameworks-guide-to-ethical-ai-implementation.

D

Data Dynamics. n.d. "Data Privacy and Security: Guardrails for Trust in a Shifting Digital World." https://www.datadynamicsinc.com/glossary-data-privacy-amp-security-guardrails-for-trust-in-a-shifting-digital-world/.

Deremuk, Iryna. 2025. "AI Ethics and Safety in 2025: Your Guide to Responsible AI Implementation." *LITSLINK* (blog), March 31. https://litslink.com/blog/ai-safety-and-ethics.

Diamandis, Peter H. 2024. "Longevity Escape Velocity: Nearing Immortality?" Blog, May 2. https://www.diamandis.com/blog/longevity-escape-velocity.

Diamond, Jared. 1997. *Guns, Germs, and Steel: The Fates of Human Societies*. W. W. Norton.

Dittmar, Jeremiah E. 2011. "Information Technology and Economic Change: The Impact of the Printing Press." *The Quarterly Journal of Economics* 126 (3): 1133–72. https://doi.org/10.1093/qje/qjr035.

Donegan, John. 2025. "Brazil Emerges as a Global Leader in Data Privacy." *ManageEngine Insights* (blog), June 10. https://insights.manageengine.com/privacy-compliance/brazil-emerges-as-a-global-leader-in-data-privacy/.

E

Eastwood, Brian. 2025. "When Humans and AI Work Best Together—and When Each Is Better Alone." *MIT Ideas Made to Matter* (blog), February 3. https://mitsloan.mit.edu/ideas-made-to-matter/when-humans-and-ai-work-best-together-and-when-each-better-alone.

Eisenstein, Elizabeth L. 1980. *The Printing Press as an Agent of Change: Communications and Cultural Transformations in Early-Modern Europe* (Vols. 1–2). Cambridge University Press.

Encyclopedia Britannica Editors. 2025. "Industrial Revolution." *Encyclopedia Britannica*, July 11, 2025. https://www.britannica.com/event/Industrial-Revolution.

EUROfusion News. 2024. "Breaking New Ground: JET Tokamak's Latest Fusion Energy Record Shows Mastery of Fusion Processes." *Eurofusion News*, February 8. https://euro-fusion.org/eurofusion-news/dte3record/.

European Commission. 2024. "AI Act." https://digital-strategy.ec.europa.eu/en/policies/regulatory-framework-ai.

F

Febvre, Lucien, and Henri-Jean Martin. 2010. *The Coming of the Book: The Impact of Printing, 1450–1800*. Translated by David Gerard. Verso Books.

Fletcher, Richard. *Echo Chambers, Filter Bubbles, and Polarisation: A Literature Review*. Oxford: Reuters Institute for the Study of Journalism, 2019.

Forsyth, Ollie. 2024. "The Creator Economy 2025." *New Economies* (Substack), October 22. https://www.neweconomies.co/p/the-creator-economy-2025.

Fessenden, Maris, and Rudy Molinek. 2024. "This Old Experiment with Mice Led to Bleak Predictions for Humanity's Future." *Smithsonian Magazine*. Originally published February 26, 2015. Updated August 8, 2024. https://www.smithsonianmag.com/

smart-news/this-old-experiment-with-mice-led-to-bleak-predictions-for-humanitys-future-180954423/.

Futrelle, D. 2023. "Is It So Wrong to Spend Two Hours a Day Chatting with Bots? How About Twelve?" *My AI Obsession* (Substack), May 11.https://www.myaiobsession.com/p/is-it-so-wrong-to-spend-two-hours.

G

Gerlich, Michael. "AI Tools in Society: Impacts on Cognitive Offloading and the Future of Critical Thinking." *Societies* 15, no. 1 (2025): 6.

Gloor, Lukas. 2023. "AI Alignment Researchers May Have a Comparative Advantage in Reducing S Risks." *Effective Altruism Forum*, February 15. https://forum.effectivealtruism.org/posts/8yaQ6i3oaFLprsFyb/ai-alignment-researchers-may-have-a-comparative-advantage-in.

Gowlett, John A. J. 2016. "The Discovery of Fire by Humans: A Long and Convoluted Process." *Philosophical Transactions of the Royal Society B* 371 (1696): 20150164. https://doi.org/10.1098/rstb.2015.0164.

Grand View Research. 2024. *Artificial Intelligence Market Size, Share & Trends Analysis Report by Solution, by Technology (Deep Learning, Machine Learning, NLP, Machine Vision, Generative AI), by Function, by End-Use, by Region, and Segment Forecasts, 2025–2030*. https://www.grandviewresearch.com/industry-analysis/artificial-intelligence-ai-market.

Graylin, Alvin Wang, and Paul Triolo. 2025. "There Can Be No Winners in a US–China AI Arms Race." *MIT Technology Review* summarized in *PYMNTS*, February 6. https://www.pymnts.com/cpi-posts/there-can-be-no-winners-in-a-us-china-ai-arms-race/.

Gupta, Lalit Mohan. 2025. "Why Purpose-Built AI Agents Are the Future of AI at Work." *Mirketa*, April 7. https://mirketa.com/purpose-built-ai-agents-agentforce/.

H

Hanauer, Nick. [TED]. 2014. "Beware, Fellow Plutocrats, the Pitchforks Are Coming" TED Talk, posted August 12. YouTube, 20:26. https://youtu.be/q2gO4DKVpa8.

Handwerk, Brian. 2020. "To Adapt to a Changing Environment 400,000 Years Ago, Early Humans Developed New Tools and Behaviors." *Smithsonian Magazine*. October 21. https://www.smithsonianmag.com/science-nature/how-drastic-ecological-change-led-leap-forward-behavior-weapons-and-tools-180976101/.

Harari, Yuval Noah. 2015. *Sapiens: A Brief History of Humankind*. Harper.

Helion Energy. 2023. "Helion Announces World's First Fusion Energy Purchase Agreement with Microsoft." May 10. https://www.helionenergy.com/articles/helion-announces-worlds-first-fusion-ppa-with-microsoft/.

Herwick, John. 2023. "12 Groundbreaking Inventions of the Industrial Revolution." *Histicle* (blog), May 18. https://histicle.com/key-inventions-of-the-industrial-revolution/.

Highland, Brittney. 2017. "Oldowan Stone Tools and Hominin Cognition." Undergraduate senior thesis, University of South Alabama. https://jagworks.southalabama.edu/anthro_ugrad_theses/14/.

Hlubik, Sarah, Francesco Berna, Craig Feibel, David Braun, and John W. K. Harris. 2017. "Researching the Nature of Fire at 1.5 MYA at FxJj20 AB, Koobi Fora, Kenya, Using High-Resolution Spatial Analysis and FTIR Spectrometry." *Current Anthropology* 58 (S16): S243–S257. https://www.journals.uchicago.edu/doi/full/10.1086/692530.

Hodges, Andrew. 1983. *Alan Turing: The Enigma*. Simon & Schuster.

Hong, Sungmin, Jean-Pierre Candelone, Clair C. Patterson, and Claude F. Boutron. 1994. "Greenland Ice Evidence of Hemispheric Lead Pollution Two Millennia Ago by Greek and Roman Civilizations." *Science* 265 (5180): 1841–43. https://www.science.org/doi/10.1126/science.265.5180.1841.

I

Ignatius, Adi. 2023. "AI Won't Replace Humans—But Humans with AI Will Replace Humans without AI." *Harvard Business Review*, August 4. https://hbr.org/2023/08/ai-wont-replace-humans-but-humans-with-ai-will-replace-humans-without-ai.

Influencer Marketing Factory. 2024. "2024 Creator Economy Predictions." January 23. https://theinfluencermarketingfactory.com/2024-creator-economy-predictions/.

Intel. 2024. "AI Education Workforce Program in the US." Accessed August 7, 2025. https://www.intel.com/content/www/us/en/corporate/artificial-intelligence/ai-for-workforce-us.html.

International Energy Agency. 2024. *Electricity 2024: Analysis and Forecast to 2026*. https://www.iea.org/reports/electricity-2024.

International Federation of Robotics (IFR). 2020. *World Robotics Report 2020. IFR Press Room*, September 24. https://ifr.org/ifr-press-releases/news/record-2.7-million-robots-work-in-factories-around-the-globe.

International IDEA (International Institute for Democracy and Electoral Assistance). 2021. "Global State of Democracy Report 2021." https://www.idea.int/gsod-2021/global-report/index.html.

J

Johns, Adrian. 1998. *The Nature of the Book: Print and Knowledge in the Making*. University of Chicago Press.

Jones, Nicola. 2018. "How to Stop Data Centres from Gobbling Up the World's Electricity." *Nature* 561 (7722): 163–166. https://www.nature.com/articles/d41586-018-06610-y.

Jyotishi, Shalin. 2024. "Community Colleges Unite to Scale AI Workforce Education." *New America* (blog), August 5. https://www.newamerica.org/education-policy/edcentral/community-colleges-unite-to-scale-ai-workforce-education/.

K

Katzke, Corin, and Gideon Futerman. 2025. "Why Racing to Artificial Superintelligence Would Undermine America's National Security." *AI Frontiers*, April 9. https://ai-frontiers.org/articles/why-racing-to-artificial-superintelligence-would-undermine-americas-national-security.

Kelly, Mark. 2025. "AI and Human Collaboration: The Future of Workplace Productivity 2025." *Mark Kelly AI*, January 3. https://markkellyai.com/ai-and-human-collaboration-the-future-of-workplace-productivity-2025/.

Kelly, Robert L. 2013. *The Lifeways of Hunter-Gatherers: The Foraging Spectrum*. Cambridge University Press.

Koulopoulos, Thomas. 2018. "According to Peter Diamandis and Ray Kurzweil, These Are the Most Dangerous and Disruptive Ideas." *Inc.*, January 19. https://www.inc.com/thomas-koulopoulos/according-to-peter-diamandis-ray-kurtzweil-this-is-how-you-build-future.html.

Kristiansen, Kristian, and Thomas B. Larsson. 2005. *The Rise of Bronze Age Society: Travels, Transmissions and Transformations*. Cambridge University Press.

L

Lapointe, Valerie A. 2024. "People Are Falling in Love with AI-Powered Romantic Chatbots. What This Says About the Future of Relationships." *ZME Science*, July 15. https://www.zmescience.com/science/people-are-falling-in-love-with-ai-powered-romantic-chatbots-what-this-says-about-the-future-of-relationships/.

Leikas, Jaana. 2018. "Ethical Artificial Intelligence as a Competitive Advantage." VTT Technical Research Centre of Finland, May 30. https://www.vttresearch.com/en/news-and-ideas/ethical-artificial-intelligence-competitive-advantage.

Lumen Learning. n.d. Neolithic Revolution. *LibreTexts Social Sciences* ccessed August 7, 2025. https://socialsci.libretexts.org/Bookshelves/Anthropology/Cultural_Anthropology/Cultural_Anthropology_%28Evans%29/07%3A_Economic_Organization/7.06%3A_Neolithic_Revolution.

Lorenz-Spreen, Philipp, Lisa Oswald, Stephan Lewandowsky, and Ralph Hertwig. "A Systematic Review of Worldwide Causal and Correlational Evidence on Digital Media and Democracy." *Nature Human Behaviour* 7, no. 1 (2023): 74-101.

Lycett, Stephen J., and John A. J. Gowlett. 2008. "On Questions Surrounding the Acheulean 'Tradition.'" *World Archaeology* 40 (3): 295–315. https://www.tandfonline.com/doi/abs/10.1080/00438240802260970.

M

Makridis, Christos. 2025. "Play the Long Game with Human-AI Collaboration." *Gallup Workplace* (blog), May 16. https://www.gallup.com/workplace/660572/play-long-game-human-ai-collaboration.aspx.

Man, John. 2002. *Gutenberg: How One Man Remade the World with Words*. Wiley.

McCartney, Scott. *ENIAC: The Triumphs and Tragedies of the World's First Computer.* New York: Walker & Company, 1999.

McNeill, John Robert. 2000. *Something New Under the Sun: An Environmental History of the Twentieth-Century World.* W. W. Norton.

Milberg, Tanya. 2024. "The Future of Learning: How AI Is Revolutionizing Education 4.0." *World Economic Forum*, April 28. https://www.weforum.org/stories/2024/04/future-learning-ai-revolutionizing-education-4-0/.

Milmo, Dan. 2025. "Former OpenAI Safety Researcher Brands Pace of AI Development 'Terrifying.'" *Guardian*, January 28. https://www.theguardian.com/technology/2025/jan/28/former-openai-safety-researcher-brands-pace-of-ai-development-terrifying.

Mokyr, J. 1990. *The Lever of Riches: Technological Creativity and Economic Progress.* Oxford University Press.

Montgomery, David R. 2007. *Dirt: The Erosion of Civilizations.* University of California Press.

Moore, Andrew M. T., Gordon C. Hillman, and Anthony J. Legge. 2000. *Village on the Euphrates: From Foraging to Farming at Abu Hureyra.* Oxford University Press.

Müller, Vincent C. 2020. "Ethics of Artificial Intelligence and Robotics." *Stanford Encyclopedia of Philosophy*, April 30. https://plato.stanford.edu/entries/ethics-ai/.

Murthy, Vivek H. 2023. *Our Epidemic of Loneliness and Isolation: The U.S. Surgeon General's Advisory on the Healing Effects of Social Connection and Community.* U.S. Department of Health and Human Services, Office of the Surgeon General. https://www.hhs.gov/sites/default/files/surgeon-general-social-connection-advisory.pdf.

N

Naithani, Sushma. 2021. *History and Science of Cultivated Plants.* Oregon State University. https://open.oregonstate.education/cultivatedplants/.

O

Open Philanthropy. 2025. "Request for Proposals: Technical AI Safety Research." https://www.openphilanthropy.org/request-for-proposals-technical-ai-safety-research/.

OpenAI. 2023. "GPT-4." Technical report, March 14. https://openai.com/research/gpt-4.

P

Perlin, John. 1991. *A Forest Journey: The Role of Wood in the Development of Civilization*. Harvard University Press.

Pfister, Rolf, and Hansueli Jud. 2025. "Understanding and Benchmarking Artificial Intelligence: OpenAI's o3 Is Not AGI." *arXiv*, January 13. https://doi.org/10.48550/arXiv.2501.07458.

Picard, Rosalind W. 2000. *Affective Computing*. MIT Press.

Pigott, Vincent C. 1999. *The Archaeometallurgy of the Asian Old World*. University of Pennsylvania Museum of Archaeology and Anthropology.

Puckett, Jim, and Smith, Ted, eds. 2002. *Exporting Harm: The High-Tech Trashing of Asia*. Basel Action Network and Silicon Valley Toxics Coalition report, February 25. https://static1.squarespace.com/static/558f1c27e4b0927589e0edad/t/55d79060e4b0ff44487f306a/1440190560888/BANsExportingHarm-2002.pdf.

R

Rau, Eli G., and Susan Stokes. 2025. "Income Inequality and the Erosion of Democracy in the Twenty-First Century." *PNAS* 122 (1): e2422543121. https://doi.org/10.1073/pnas.2422543121.

Redman, Charles L. 1999. *Human Impact on Ancient Environments*. University of Arizona Press.

The Register. "Brain Activity Lower When Using AI Chatbots: MIT Research." June 18, 2024. https://www.theregister.com/2025/06/18/is_ai_changing_our_brains/.

Riordan, Michael, and Lillian Hoddeson. 1997. *Crystal Fire: The Birth of the Information Age*. W. W. Norton.

Romeo, Zaira, and Alberto Testolin. 2025. "Artificial Intelligence Can Emulate Human Normative Judgments on Emotional Visual Scenes." *arXiv*, March 24. https://doi.org/10.48550/arXiv.2503.18796.

S

Samuel, Sigal. 2025. "AI Is Impersonating Human Therapists. Can It Be Stopped?" *Vox Future Perfect*, February 10. https://www.vox.com/future-perfect/398905/ai-therapy-chatbots-california-bill.

Sartre, Jean-Paul. 2007. *Existentialism Is a Humanism*. Translated by Carol Macomber. Yale University Press.

Sawhney, Inderpreet, Delia Ferriera Rubio, and Houssam Al Wazzan. 2024. "Why Corporate Integrity Is Key to Shaping Future Use of AI." World Economic Forum. October 14. https://www.weforum.org/stories/2024/10/corporate-integrity-future-ai-regulation/

Seo, Jaemin, Sang Kyeun Kim, Azarakhsh Jalalvand, et al. 2024. "Avoiding Fusion Plasma Tearing Instability with Deep Reinforcement Learning." *Nature* 626: 746–751. https://doi.org/10.1038/s41586-024-07024-9.

Sevak, Amit. 2025. "Four Ways to Enhance Human-AI Collaboration in the Workplace." *World Economic Forum*, January 13. https://www.weforum.org/stories/2025/01/four-ways-to-enhance-human-ai-collaboration-in-the-workplace/.

Shear, Emmett. *Superintelligence Is Coming, Here's How Humanity Survives*. YouTube video, 10:03. Posted by *YouTube*. Accessed August 15. https://www.youtube.com/watch?v=uFQFIGyD6FE.

Silver, David, Aja Huang, Chris J. Maddison, et al. 2016. "Mastering the Game of Go with Deep Neural Networks and Tree Search." *Nature* 529: 484–89. https://doi.org/10.1038/nature16961.

Sinek, Simon. 2019. *The Infinite Game.* Portfolio.

Slashdot. 2025. "Brazil Tests Letting Citizens Earn Money from Data in Their Digital Footprint." *Slashdot*, May 31. https://yro.slashdot.org/story/25/06/01/0222237/brazil-tests-letting-citizens-earn-money-from-data-in-their-digital-footprint.

Smith, Bruce D. 1995. *The Emergence of Agriculture*. W. H. Freeman.

Son, Kihoon, Jinhyeon Kwon, DaEun Choi, et al. 2024. "Unveiling Disparities in Web Task Handling Between Human and Web Agent." *arXiv*, May 7. https://doi.org/10.48550/arXiv.2405.04497.

Sparks, Hannah. New York Post. 2025. "Mini 'Artificial Sun' Sets New Record—the Closest Earth Has Come to Achieving Limitless Clean Energy." *New York Post*, January 22. https://nypost.com/2025/01/22/science/artificial-sun-sets-new-record-toward-goal-of-limitless-clean-energy/.

Stauffer, Nancy W. (MIT Energy Initiative). 2024. "More Durable Metals for Fusion Power Reactors." *MIT News*, August 19. https://news.mit.edu/2024/more-durable-metals-fusion-power-reactors-0819.

Stout, Dietrich. 2011. "Stone Toolmaking and the Evolution of Human Culture and Cognition." *Philosophical Transactions of the Royal Society B*, 366 (1567): 1050–59. https://royalsocietypublishing.org/doi/10.1098/rstb.2010.0369.

Sumner, Michael. 2024. "Blockchain for Music Royalties: 2024 Guide." *ScoreDetect* (blog), May 23. https://www.scoredetect.com/blog/posts/blockchain-for-music-royalties-2024-guide.

Swade, Doron. 2000. *The Difference Engine: Charles Babbage and the Quest to Build the First Computer*. Viking.

T

Taylor, Khari, and Nicholas Diakopoulos. "Artificial Intelligence and Democracy: Pathway to Progress or Decline?" *Journal of Information Technology & Politics* 22, no. 1 (2025): 1-15.

Thompson, E. P. 1963. *The Making of the English Working Class*. Victor Gollancz Ltd.

Todd, Benjamin. 2025. "It Looks Like There Are Some Good Funding Opportunities in AI Safety Right Now." *80,000 Hours* (blog), January 10. https://80000hours.org/2025/01/it-looks-like-there-are-some-good-funding-opportunities-in-ai-safety-right-now/.

Tom's Hardware. 2025. "AI Experts Warn That China Is Miles Ahead of the U.S. in Electricity Generation." *Tom's Hardware News*, August 15, 2025.

Toole, Betty A. 1992. *Ada, the Enchantress of Numbers: Prophet of the Computer Age*. Strawberry Press.

Topol, Eric. 2019. *Deep Medicine: How Artificial Intelligence Can Make Healthcare Human Again*. Basic Books.

Turing, Alan M. 1936. On Computable Numbers, with an Application to the Entscheidungsproblem." Proceedings of the London Mathematical Society, s2-42 (1): 230–265. https://doi.org/10.1112/plms/s2-42.1.230.

Turing, Alan M. 1950. "Computing Machinery and Intelligence." *Mind* 49: 433–460. https://doi.org/10.1093/mind/LIX.236.433.

U

US Department of Energy. 2025. "AI Tackles Disruptive Tearing Instability in Fusion Plasma." *Fusion Energy Sciences*, January 3. https://www.energy.gov/science/fes/articles/ai-tackles-disruptive-tearing-instability-fusion-plasma.

US National Science Foundation. n.d. "Advancing Ethical Artificial Intelligence through the Power of Convergent Research." Accessed August 7, 2025. https://www.nsf.gov/funding/initiatives/nrt/advancing-ethical-ai-through-convergent-research.

V

Vaswani, Ashish, Noam Shazeer, Niki Parmar, et al. 2017. "Attention Is All You Need." *Advances in Neural Information Processing Systems* 30. https://arxiv.org/abs/1706.03762.

W

Wang, Senhu, Lambert Zixin Li, and Adam Coutts. 2022. National Survey of Mental Health and Life Satisfaction of Gig Workers: The Role of Loneliness and Financial Precarity." *BMJ Open* 12 (12): e066389. https://doi.org/10.1136/bmjopen-2022-066389.

Warner, Helen. 2023. "Review: Star Trek and Humanism." South East London Humanist Group. https://selondon.humanist.org.uk/review-star-trek-and-humanism/.

Wilkins, Jayne. 2020. "Learner-Driven Innovation in the Stone Tool Technology of Early *Homo sapiens*." *Evolutionary Human Sciences* 2: 1–17. https://doi.org/10.1017/ehs.2020.40.

Wilkinson, Freddie. 2025. "Industrialization, Labor and Life." *National Geographic Education*, May 30. https://education.nationalgeographic.org/resource/industrialization-labor-and-life.

Wilson, H. James, and Paul R. Daugherty. 2018. "Collaborative Intelligence: Humans and AI Are Joining Forces." *Harvard Business Review*, July–August. https://hbr.org/2018/07/collaborative-intelligence-humans-and-ai-are-joining-forces.

World Economic Forum. 2024. *Navigating the AI Frontier: A Primer on the Evolution and Impact of AI Agents*. https://reports.weforum.org/docs/WEF_Navigating_the_AI_Frontier_2024.pdf.

World Economic Forum. 2025. *The Future of Jobs Report 2025*. January 7. https://www.weforum.org/publications/the-future-of-jobs-report-2025/.

Wrangham, Richard. 2009. *Catching Fire: How Cooking Made Us Human.* Basic Books.

Wray, Sarah. 2025. "Brazilian Pilot Explores Letting Citizens Control—and Sell—Their Personal Data." *Global Government Forum*, October 6. https://www.globalgovernmentforum.com/brazilian-pilot-explores-letting-citizens-control-and-sell-their-personal-data/.

Wynn, Thomas. 1995. "Handaxe Enigmas." *World Archaeology* 27 (1): 10–24. http://www.jstor.org/stable/124775.

X

XzERp. 2025. "Your Data Is Worth $50/Month—Brazil Proves It" Video, posted June 1. YouTube, 8:55. https://www.youtube.com/watch?v=rcjbX5faJ4M.

Y

Yonck, Richard. 2017. *Heart of the Machine: Our Future in a World of Artificial Emotional Intelligence*. Arcade Publishing.

Z

Zeder, Melinda A. 2008. "Domestication and Early Agriculture in the Mediterranean Basin: Origins, Diffusion, and Impact. *PNAS* 105 (33): 11597–11604. https://doi.org/10.1073/pnas.0801317105.

ZME Science. 2024. "People Are Falling in Love with AI-Powered Romantic Chatbots—What This Says about the Future of Relationships." July 15, 2024. *ZME Science*.

ABOUT THE AUTHOR

Zac Engler is a Minnesota-born futurist, AI strategist, and founder of Bodhi AI, a consultancy that helps businesses harness artificial intelligence to scale smarter and lead with confidence.

He began writing about AI in 2016, when he recognized just how quickly the technology was advancing and how few people truly understood what was coming. Armed with curiosity, a passion for history, and a relentless drive to learn, he devoured books on everything from physics to philosophy and machine learning. Many of his early predictions about AI's evolution have already been proven correct.

Zac is a self-starter who's built his career from the ground up. This drive has taken him from scrappy blog posts to the cutting edge of AI development, where he now works as Chief AI Officer at C4 Technical Services. Along the way, he's built high-performing teams at companies like Apple, Amplifon, and Sanctuary AI, and led executive searches across healthcare, automation, and advanced tech.

More than anything, Zac cares about people. He wants to help readers understand the tidal wave of AI that's approaching and show them how to ride it rather than be swept away.

Turning On Machines combines hard-won insights, real-world experience, and a deep respect for the past to challenge how we think about technology. It's a call to action for leaders to step up, stay human, and rewire the future before it rewires them.

zacengler.com